As an avid movie enthusiast, I can usually guess the end of any ...,
no matter how many plot twists. For over forty years, I have heard
sermons and read works by countless scholars and theologians on the
life of Joseph. I have even written and preached every revelation from
the pit to the palace, or so I thought. In all my preaching experience,
nothing was beyond the palace. I made it to the palace with Joseph, but
I never looked out of a door or window beyond what I thought to be
God's ultimate purpose.

The good news is that God has a plan for our lives, and often His plan
is incomprehensible; His ways are so beyond us. In *Beyond the Palace*,
Smith has thoroughly labored to open the door of our hearts to God's
all-encompassing, incredibly awesome sovereignty. This time, I did
not see it coming.

Jimmy Sneed
Founder and Pastor
Rivers of Living Water Church
Albany, Georgia

Clayton D. Smith is one of the most prolific writers of this century.
Due to its scholarly approach, *Beyond the Palace* could be taught in
the academy, but because of its spiritual truths, it could be taught as a
lesson at church. This is a great read, and all will be glad that we inhale
the fresh air from *Beyond the Palace*.

Lorenzo Heard
Senior Pastor
Greater 2nd Mt. Olive Baptist Church
Albany, Georgia

Pastor Clayton Smith has truly written a prophetic, progressive,
revelatory book on the life of Joseph. As I read these twelve power-
packed chapters, each chapter leading beautifully into the other reveals
the providential care and provision of our God. The author's insight

concerning Psalms 105:17, when our Father says he "sent a man even Joseph," gave a new framework of understanding. It was powerful as I read each chapter, knowing that at every stage of Joseph's life, regardless of his circumstances, he was "sent" by God, and God was using those circumstances for His glory. This divinely inspired book is a must-read.

The book of Genesis teaches us that when Joseph revealed himself to his brothers after their betrayal, he said to them, "But as for you, you meant evil against me; but God meant it for good, in order to bring it about as it is this day, to save many people alive" (Genesis 50:20). We see how this perspective is what made Joseph such a powerful man. He saw that even though what his brothers did was evil and wrong, God still used it to bring about something miraculous for them and the nation of Israel. Notice that the passage reads: "... as it is this day." However, "this day," took a few years, but it finally came. The author reminds us we must be patient. We must trust Father. God is using everything, no matter what it looks like right now.

Romans 8:28 says, "And we know that all things work together for good to those who love God, to those who are the called according to His purpose." In this time and this hour, when people are trying to figure everything out, and get their life back to what it was, God is trying to move our lives to something so much better. God can use our pits, prisons, and brokenness to propel us to our destiny.

We know that some really bad things have happened in our world. God does not "cause" all things. He does not cause disease, tragedy, and negative things. Yet, God can use those things and shape them with purpose and meaning. God can take the good and the bad; He can take our hills and valleys (1 Kings 29:28). And through the power of the cross and His Word, He causes these things to result in something good.

Let us remember that God is not just the author of our faith. He is the finisher, too (Heb. 12: 2). Pastor Smith thoroughly reminds us to trust Father to finish the work He has begun. Let us also remember that God is with us in the valleys as well as in the mountains. He never leaves us or forsakes us. Surely, His goodness and mercy follow us (wherever we are) all the days of our lives (Psalm 23).

From the beginning to the very end of this book, we come to realize what it means to be called by God truly, and to answer that call, as did this dreamer, Joseph.

Joe J. Brock
Pastor, Cutting Edge Ministries Church
President, Advocate Ministries, Inc.
Birmingham, Alabama

BEYOND THE PALACE

BEYOND THE PALACE

THE IMPLICATIONS OF JOSEPH'S DREAMS

CLAYTON D. SMITH

Bridgeport, CT 06605
www.hovpub.com

Beyond the Palace
The Implications of Joseph's Dreams

HOV Publishing a division of HOV, LLC.
Bridgeport, CT 06605
Email: hopeofvision@gmail.com / www.hovpub.com

Cover Design and inside text design/layout by Hope of Vision Designs
Editor: Clayton D. Smith
Proofreaders: Yelena Arrington, Jaime Belk, and Genesis Literary Indulgence Editing Services

Contact the Author: Clayton D. Smith at: cdsmith3230@gmail.com

For further information regarding special discounts on bulk purchases, please contact: Clayton D. Smith at cdsmith3230@gmail.com

ISBN Paperback: 978-1-955107-63-1
ISBN eBook: 978-1-955107-62-4

Cataloging-in-Publication data is on file with The Library of Congress.
LCCN:

Printed in the United States of America

To my beloved family, the Bread of Life Church, who gave me leave for months to pray and write this book. To my mother, Patricia Smith, a true image-bearer, who taught me to love the Lord and has exampled Christ all my life. To Yelena Arrington, my sister, and Jaime Belk, my daughter in Christ, who suffered through hours editing this work. To Dr. Lillian Sneed, my technical consultant and inspiration. To the body of Christ as we eagerly long for His appearing. Most importantly, to the glory of God.

CONTENTS

FOREWORD

Dr. Clayton Smith has written an insightful book on the person of Joseph in the Book of Genesis. Dr. Smith has explored the personal, theological, and eschatological implications of the character of Joseph. The author of this work weaves the supernatural hand of God upon Joseph in his young teenage years. The book's writer explores how God works behind and providentially in the scenes of those He chooses for His glory and honor that are keen to His majesty in its value.

Dr. Smith captures well Joseph's walk with God even with the young man not completely understanding the immediate implications of His dream and the reasons of His odyssey in Egypt as a prisoner when he was betrayed and sold by His brothers. The disdain of his brothers brought Joseph to the point of being mistreated horribly. The author captures well the tangential meanings of Joseph's story.

The author weaves Joseph's experience of God's hand in his life difficulties. He argues that God does not always keep us from evil but protects us even while in it honing our faith however disheartening things may appear (Rom. 1:17). The writer discusses the larger implications of God's own and their plight as He develops their character through trial (John 16:33). The book's author weaves well the lack of celebrity of a child of God (James 2:5) that he she does not receive from the world (John 15:18-19). Such is similar to Christ who came to those who were His own people, but He was dismissed and considered valueless (Is. 53:4, John 1:11).

Joseph would languish in prison, the author writes, as his father grieved over his reported death. Dr. Smith paints well that the methods of God are not visible success but an inner trust and calm for those called by Him are called to trust Him beyond what they see (2 Cor 4:18). All that Joseph needed was God despite the act of His brothers. Reuben and Judah, his brothers, acted to keep him from dying and Judah promised to bring His younger brother Benjamin back home to his father Jacob.

Dr. Smith discusses the favor that Joseph would receive from Potiphar despite his having been a prisoner and slave. The writer conveys how protective and providential God's hand was upon Joseph despite how dismal things seemed. The author tells how Joseph survived the accusations of Potiphar's wife while winding up in prison again. The writer continually conveys how God constantly protected His dreamer.

As the author reminds the reader, the Lord does not forsake His own. God does not forsake His children. The book's writer makes the consistent point that God protects His dreamer no matter what they face (Heb. 13:5). Dr. Smith constantly reinforces the point that God will guide His called through the most harrowing of circumstances. The writer makes this point consistently and continuously throughout the book that God will not forsake the faithful (2 Tim. 2:11-13).

So, if you want a good read concerning God's providential guidance and power no matter what issue His servant faces you will enjoy this book. A reader can take great solace in the fact that just as God protected Joseph through prison as he would ultimately become a high governmental official in a foreign land (Gen. 41:40), He can and will deliver and exalt His own. Joseph's brothers, father, Israel, and the nations of history have benefited from God's hand upon his life down to his greatest ancestor Jesus Christ the Savior of the world (Gen. 45:7).

What Dr. Smith does is that he molds and shapes well in this book three great themes they are: God loves His own, He is always at work despite the circumstance, and His goal is deliverance of believer(s) in Him for His glory. The writer always looks and considers God's wide view through this work. This is a great book displaying God's providence in Joseph's life and ultimately each of our lives. This book will inspire and encourage you to run on and finish your race well for Christ, like the Apostle Paul wrote: 2 Timothy 4:7-8 "I have fought the good fight, I have finished the race, I have kept the faith. Finally, there is laid up for me the crown of righteousness, which the Lord, the righteous Judge, will give to me on that Day, and not to me only but also to all who have loved His appearing".

Dennis McDonald, PhD
Assistant Professor
Liberty University

INTRODUCTION

The story of Joseph has always been one of my favorite stories in the Bible. God gave a young man, Joseph, a gift, but the gift was a mystery to him and woefully misunderstood by Joseph's family, perhaps arguably so. It caused such animosity among his brothers that they hated him unto death. They were even willing to allow their father, who loved Joseph beyond words, to grieve himself almost to the grave. To be called out and chosen by God is truly a blessing, but with the blessing of chosenness comes the burden of responsibility, which sometimes may seem unfair and unbearable.

Joseph did receive divinely inspired dreams; however, the Lord did not show him the full import of his assignment. The terrible things that happened to Joseph because of his prophetic dreams he could not see coming. Of course, when the giver is God, who among us can fully comprehend His all-encompassing omniscience and His divine sovereignty? God's "understanding is inscrutable" (Isa. 40:28), His judgments are unsearchable and unfathomable (Rom. 11:33-44), and His ways are so beyond human comprehension (Isa. 55:8-9).

I have heard the story of Joseph preached many times over the years. The pit to the palace is usually the scope, with Joseph's elevation to the palace as the pinnacle. However, I have never heard anyone preach about the implications of Joseph's calling, life, and dreams beyond the palace. This story is replete with themes such as unconditional love, integrity, endurance, and forgiveness, but the most prominent theological theme among them is the providence of God. In this narrative, we witness God's sometimes invisible yet meticulous hand in the lives and destinies of His people to accomplish His mission on earth.

In retrospect, we see the providential hand of God at work from the first mention of his dreams to his family until he reached the palace in Egypt. We can see God at work in the dingy pit, Potiphar's house, Joseph's stint in prison, and his elevation to the palace. However, what about afterward? What could the significance of Joseph's dreams mean beyond Egypt? God had a plan; He has always had a divine plan since the beginning of human existence.

While it is climactic, to say the least, it is not the ultimate. The palace in Egypt is not the culmination of God's plans and purposes. It reaches us today from the preservation and creation of a nation, God's chosen people, to Jesus Christ. Furthermore, it continues to unfold as we await the coming of our Lord and Redeemer. The eschatological implications of Joseph's dreams are far-reaching, climaxing at the day our Lord shall appear, thus, the final destiny of our souls, our eternal destiny.

Remember, absolutely nothing happens outside of God's authority, and He is in complete control no matter how things look, sound, or feel.

CHAPTER 1

From the Dream to the Pit

God told Jeremiah, "Before I formed you in the womb, I knew you; before you were born, I set you apart; I appointed you as a prophet to the nations" (Jer. 1:5 NIV). Loved by his father and loathed by his brothers, it appears Joseph is no exception. God called him to do what God only chose him to do. From the beginning of this biblical drama, it is apparent that the life of Joseph is destined for greatness. He is a dreamer. At age seventeen, he was a prophetic dreamer. Although his immediate family was the focal point of his dreams, little to his knowledge, the dreams had far-reaching implications. In other words, what God had in mind was far greater than Joseph's narrow interpretation and his life experience.

God's plans and purposes are sometimes beyond human comprehension. Whatever we dream, desire, think, or imagine pales compared to what God can do (Eph. 3:20). God's desires for us are far greater than we could ever hope for ourselves. Regardless of your hopes, dreams, and desires, God's heart for you is always larger than your aspirations for yourself.

Paul quotes from Isaiah 55:8-9, "Who has known the mind of the Lord?" (Rom. 11:34). God's ways and thoughts are truly on a different plateau than ours. Man's concept of advancement and elevation is often through aggressive and sometimes ruthless behavior. However, God's plan of elevation and advancement for His children or His will is by way of humility. For example, Peter advises, "Humble yourselves, therefore, under God's mighty hand, that He may lift you up in due time" (1 Pet.5:6). To the church at Colossae, Paul instructs the "elect of God" or the believer to "clothe yourselves with compassion, kindness, humility, gentleness, and patience" (Col. 3:12). To the church at Corinth, Paul declares, "no one knows the thoughts of God except the Spirit of God" (1 Cor. 2:11).

Not only is Joseph to save his family, but the entire world from utter disaster. The truth is that the dream is always bigger than the dreamer and sometimes even the dreamer's capacity to comprehend its intricacies. However, the plans and purposes of God are never frustrated by one's inabilities or inadequacies. God never has to make a dream to fit the man; He makes the man to fit the dream. He does not call you because of who you are. Instead, He calls you because of the treasure He has placed within you and who He knows you will become (2 Tim. 1:14). As such, God stretches and strengthens you for the assignment. Like Joseph, God will raise you to meet the task.

One can only imagine that carrying such a gift from God at so early an age is challenging for several reasons. First, he is young and probably immature. Bezalel Naor suggests, "There is incredible naïveté in Joseph narrating to his brothers his dreams of grandeur."[1] Honestly, Joseph had nowhere to put such an enormous revelation. He did not have the wisdom of Mary, the mother of Jesus, who, when she learned of her calling, "treasured up all these things and pondered them in her heart" (Lk. 2:19).

Second, Russell Handel suggests that "the brothers regarded Joseph's dreams as purely personal fantasies dealing with his own inner world."[2] Thus, he was already reviled by his brothers. Why did he not know that revealing his unique gift would only add fuel to the proverbial fire?

Third, there is no way that Joseph fully comprehended what God was trying to convey. Handel further suggests that "Prophetic dreams are frequently non-transparent not only in development but also in content." Therefore, "the referents of the dream objects are not immediately known. Rather, the meaning eventually becomes clear."[3] God progressively unfolds His plans and purposes, and He reveals their portion to carry out His will to every individual.

Like all who have been chosen and called by God, Joseph needed to spend time with God. Nothing prepares one to serve God more than living and resting in His holy presence. No matter what God calls one to do, nothing replaces quality time with God, much like Moses on the backside of the Midian desert (see Ex.3) or Isaiah when He received the revelation of God (Isa. 6).

The answer is Joseph was only a seventeen-year-old young man "who enjoyed telling on his siblings (Gen. 37:2),"[4] and in some cultures, he would be considered a boy. He did as most enthusiastic seventeen-year-olds, and even some gifted adults would probably do. Joseph shared his dreams with people who could never dream with him. The implications of the dreams were enormous, but his brothers were small men. He opened his heart to people who were incapable of celebrating him. They were small-minded bitter men who despised him. Thus, their hearts were dark. They were the very people with whom he should have been able to share anything; they were his brothers. If there ever was a dysfunctional family, his was a textbook case.

Nevertheless, his gift was not the only thing that got him in trouble. The extraordinary love of his father only magnified and intensified the hatred of his brothers because of the gift of which he seemingly bragged. Yes, they hated him because of it. Given a unique "coat of many colors" (Gen. 37:3) which signified a special place in his father's affection, his brothers despised Joseph unto death. Thus, they conspired to kill him.

Instead, one of his brothers, Reuben, convinced them to throw him in a pit; Reuben secretly held the hope of coming back to rescue Joseph and "deliver him to his father again" (Gen. 37:22). Joseph was stripped of his coat, then, ruthlessly, and dastardly thrown into a pit with no water or any sustenance; he was left to die. It is only through God's providential grace through Reuben that Joseph's life was spared, so to speak.

On the one hand, their blinding and binding hate for Joseph explains why they did not hesitate to conspire against him and how they could live for so many years without a hint of remorse for what they had done. On the other hand, how astoundingly depraved were his brothers, who took no thought of the unbearable grief and pain such a loss would cause their father? What Joseph's brothers felt for him was beyond jealousy or envy. They "hated him" because of their father's exceptional love for him (Gen. 37:4), and they "hated him all the more because of his dreams" (Gen. 37:8), not to mention the seemingly arrogant and presumptuous nature of the dreams or at least what they perceived to be Joseph's interpretation. Kurt Eisen posits, "Joseph may be guilty of failures in tact, but he is nonetheless the innocent victim of his brothers' resentment."[5]

Who could have imagined that this favorite son and up-and-coming prophetic voice would end up in a pit? Were his dreams of God, or were they merely dreams or delusions of grandeur? God anointed him and gave him the dreams. If so, God would indeed keep this young man from all hurt, harm, and danger. No evil would befall him that appears out of sorts, and undoubtedly, nothing adverse would happen to him that would look different from other so-called dreamers. Wrong! That is how many believers erroneously determine the hand of God or that God has blessed a thing. Those who do not know God's motif assume that all good is God and all bad is the devil. They view all good, pleasant, and convenient things as a sign of God's approval, and anything that is terrible, ugly, and inconvenient to them, indicates the devil's work.

Consequently, the church has drifted so far from biblical truth and revelation that she is hardly recognizable. For instance, even in a pandemic, the goal is to rush back into the four walls we call the church to "serve the Lord." How have we so missed the obvious? The church is more significant than a building. How do we not recognize the success of the first-century church that met from house to house (Acts 2:46) and whose work was unmistakably and inarguably Kingdom driven and approved?

Another example of a departure from biblical truth and revelation is how Evangelicals would rather fight, plot, and scheme in the political arena rather than trust God in a Kingdom reality. For example, I saw a bumper sticker that read, "Let's pray to **end** abortion." I shook my head and declared I would never join them in prayer to end abortion. That is correct, never. However, I will enthusiastically join them in prayer for biblical Christians to **begin** to make disciples as our Lord commanded.

Oh, how we have woefully missed God. Jesus said, "make disciples" (Mt. 28:19), not legislation. The truth is you cannot legislate morality. Most assuredly, those who have been discipled are less likely to turn to abortion. Perhaps if we trust God enough to cease disfiguring His church and distorting His message, abortions will end. You can change a law, but ultimately a law does not change a heart. Neither does a law save a soul.

Why, then, has the Christian church forsaken our mandate? We must renew our faith to obey God's will and join Him in His mission. Again, those who have been discipled (born again) learn to trust Him, obey Him, and, even more, seek to please and live for Him.

Nevertheless, my prayer is that the people of God will learn to trust and obey the simple commands God has already given His church.

Further, success for many believers today is defined and equated to a dome and a Bentley. A ministry's success is measured by the number of people we preach to and retain rather than how many we prepare and release to do the work of ministry. We should be sending people out, not keeping them in for the Sunday morning evangelistic hour. The gathered church is "to equip His people for the works of service, so that the body of Christ may be built up until we all reach unity in the faith and the knowledge of the Son of God and become mature" (Eph. 4:12-13).

For the immature believer, or modern church, the day Joseph, the prophetic dreamer, ended up in a pit would be the day we dismiss him as a false prophet and propagate the rumor like the first shot of the Revolutionary War. The news and judgment that Joseph is a false prophet would be heard around the world. At best, we would conclude that he had fallen from grace and had messed up with God, just as Job's friends wrongly discerned of him (see Job 4:3-4; 4:7-8; 8:20).

Likewise, many modern-day believers, the pie in the sky, name it and claim it crowd would have walked away from David. One day he is anointed king by the prophet Samuel because God said, "he is the one" (1 Sam. 16). What a massive parade to the palace. Look at the mighty and impressive army, the chariots, horses, and horsemen in shining armor as they followed behind him. What about the political elite who came out to welcome and wish him well? That banquet, oh my, what an extravagant feast King Saul set up in David's honor. Can you see the royal robe and royal jewels?

That is definitely how a man whom God has anointed would enter his new kingdom, so says the church today. After all, that is how we measure Kingdom success. Wrong again! After that anointing ceremony, David had to run for his life, hide in caves, and feign insanity. The only crowd he attracted was "All those who were in distress or in debt or discontented" (2 Sam 22:1). There was no parade, no one welcomed him, and no coronation or inaugural dinner in his honor. It is at that very point that many in today's church would have walked away from David and declared Samuel a false prophet. Thus, one of the most widely loved and memorized biblical passages, "The Lord is my shepherd; I shall not want" (Ps. 23:1 KJV), would never have made the best sellers list.

For years Joseph and David looked like failures, and I do not doubt that modern believers would not be discerning enough to stick around long. The prophetic dream was thirteen years old before Joseph reached anything resembling success, and David had no measure of what we call a success for at least fifteen years. The church would have missed God in the most significant way.

Back to Joseph. Look at the dreamer now. The pit rendered the dream impossible. The dream, along with the dreamer, is in a hole. Let us be honest. That deep dark hole looked nothing like the dream he had. It just did not look like God at all. The pit was in no way a part of Joseph's dream. The prophetic dream was that his family would bow before him. However, in real life, Joseph looks up at them from a hole in the ground, and they look down upon him.

Many people dream, but not all dreams are of God. God-dreams cost. For some, the cost is too great; the price is too high. God-dreams call for sacrifice. Joseph, this favored son, is now stripped of his unique garment, which not only reminded him of who he was to his father, but others would know the depth of his father's love for him by that coat. To his brothers, the elegant coat served as a painful reminder.

Further, He is estranged from the closeness and affection of his father. One can only imagine young Joseph's fear of never seeing his father again. Even more disturbing is the thought that his father may never know what happened to him. Now he knows. The stark reality must have set in if there was any doubt in his mind about how much they hated him. If there was any hope for the love and affirmation of his brothers, it is now clear that it would never happen. The gift of God cost him everything dear to him. God-dreams cost.

From all indications, his dreams and expectations were dashed. It was the end of the dream and the dreamer. Or was it? Joseph did not fall into the pit; he was pushed. Although their actions were hideous, heartbreaking, and hurtful, the push into the pit was, in fact, a push into his destiny. Remember, God's ways are not like our ways. Perhaps Judah would save the day.

CHAPTER 2

From the Pit to Potiphar's House

I can think of several occasions when my greatest disappointments and attacks were caused by my friends and loved ones rather than my foes. It is usually those whom we take into our affections that harm us, inflicting the most incredible pain. Most of us do not allow so-called known enemies or naysayers close enough to our hearts to make a difference. They are the ones we watch or avoid, as the case may be, not friends and family. Thus, his brothers, not strangers, pushed Joseph. He did not fall into the pit; they pushed him. Sometimes the pain is sharper, deeper, and more pronounced because of the who rather than the what. After all, they were his siblings, blood brothers, his father's sons, raised in the same household.

However, little did they know, they pushed him right where he needed to be, though hurtful it was. To them and us, it looked like a pit of death and destruction—the end of dream and dreamer, but in a spiritual reality, the dreadful hole was a vehicle of destiny. Remember, God's way is not always our way, and sometimes His ways do not make sense to us. It is the Lord who makes "your enemies a footstool for your feet" (Ps. 110:1).

Several truths begin to unfold early in this drama that we must never forget. God is always in charge. Absolutely nothing happens outside of His authority; no matter how it looks, He is in complete control. God can use anything and anyone to accomplish His will, and nothing can thwart the plans and purposes of God. Though he remains complicit because he did not tell his father, Reuben had a brush with a half conscience. God used him to convince them to spare Joseph's life (as if he would not eventually die in the pit).

However, Judah went the extra mile. He convinced his brothers to "sell him to the Ishmaelites" (Gen. 37:26). To be clear, neither Reuben nor Judah was free of guilt because they did not do the right thing. Although Joseph's life was spared because of their actions, they were both complicit. It is tempting here to say that, for whatever reason, he was not left to die in a cistern. However, there is a reason that we will discuss later (see Chapter 10). Remember, God is in complete control. He is always in control of situations, circumstances, people, and things.

Nevertheless, rather than leaving him to die, Joseph is sold by his brothers into slavery. Either way, it appears that Joseph is done. They could never take him back to his father after acting on such a conspiracy, and at this point, they were just as committed as a thumb in a slamming car door. His brothers were committed to his demise, but God was faithful to his destiny. They sold him to the Ishmaelites, who passed them on their way to Egypt to sell "spices, balm, and myrrh" (Gen. 37:25). Upon their arrival, they sold Joseph "to Potiphar, one of Pharaoh's officials, the captain of the guard" (Gen. 37:36).

A recurring theme and probably one of the most significant revelations in the story and life of Joseph is, "The Lord was with Joseph" (Gen. 39:2). Not only that, but God gave him favor enough that he lived (as an enslaved person) in the big house, Potiphar, his master's house. Yes, he was betrayed by his brothers, put into a pit, then sold into slavery, but the Lord was with him. Nothing is more comforting in life to a believer than knowing that the Lord is with you.

Whatever the situation, whatever the circumstance, if God is with you, you can make it. Paul declares, "If God is for us, who can be against us?" (Rom. 8:31). There is no stopping or blocking our path with God on our side. Thus, it is God who charts our course (Prov. 16:9). Even before birth, "before the creation of the world," God "chose us in Him" (Eph. 1:4). Therefore, God and God alone determines our destiny. There is no weapon, no force that can alter the plans and purposes of God for your life.

Although some may plot and scheme, weapons formed against you will not prevail, and God will refute every evil word spoken against you (Isa. 54:17). It was Charles Spurgeon who said, "You have not the world, but you have the Maker of the world; that is far more." He continued, "Whatever is to come of our life is in our heavenly Father's hand."[1]

Joseph was stripped of his coat of many colors, but they could not deny him what God put inside him. The coat did not make him; he made the coat. The coat was distinctively unique, and its meaning was significant, but who was in the coat was more important than the coat itself. They put him in the pit, but the pit did not get in him. They sold him into slavery, but he never had the mind of an enslaved person.

Although Joseph was a long way from his father, it did not change who he was, nor did it change what he knew about himself. Joseph was his daddy's boy and knew who he was because his daddy affirmed him. There is nothing like the affirmation of a father. Not only that, but God's hand was upon his life. If we walk with the Lord as "dearly loved children" (Eph. 5:1), like Jacob, God will let you know who you are and whose you are.

Many believers desire and celebrate confirmation, but more than anything, we need affirmation. Confirmation is from without, but affirmation is from within. Our Kingdom journey and success in life rests upon the inner strength given by God the Father through God the Son, nurtured by God the Holy Spirit. For instance, when John baptized Jesus, God affirmed Him as He spoke from heaven, saying, "This is My Son, whom I love; with Him, I am well pleased" (Mt. 3:17). Undoubtedly, the sonship of Jesus was challenged from His birth to the cross. Still today, some question the authenticity of His deity and even the historicity of His existence. Nevertheless, how did things work out for Jesus after God's affirmation? He turned the world upside down, salvation for those who believe is secured, and life everlasting awaits those who trust Him.

Joseph is now a slave in the house of Potiphar, but God gave him favor in the eyes of his new master. Remember that Joseph was no longer wearing the distinguishing coat of many colors. His brothers ripped it from his body and dredged it with blood to prove to his father that a wild animal had killed Joseph (Gen. 37:31-33). So, there was no external indication of his greatness and of who or what he was. To Potiphar, Joseph was merely a slave. However, that God was with him is not to be overlooked or understated. It means more than the world against you when God is with you. Regardless of your circumstances, God's presence assures His grace and glory upon your life.

Not only was God with Joseph, but God caused him to prosper. It is as if everything he touched turned to gold. There is no suggestion that Potiphar knew Joseph's God, but Joseph's God knew Potiphar. He "saw that the Lord was with him and that the Lord gave him success in everything he did" (Gen. 39:3). Even more, "Joseph found favor in his eyes and became his attendant. Potiphar put him in charge of his household, and he entrusted to his care everything he owned" (Gen. 39:4). The hand of God was upon Joseph so much so that the blessings of the Lord extended to Potiphar's entire house and business. Thus, "Potiphar left everything he had in Joseph's care; with Joseph in charge, he did not concern himself with anything except the food he ate" (Gen 39:6). What a step up from the pit.

It is here that everything changed for Joseph when Potiphar's wife falsely accused him of attempted rape. To this point, everything keeps changing in his life, and that is a mild statement. Of course, she lied on Joseph because he had the veracity, even more, the audacity to refuse her repeated offer of sex. She was perhaps humiliated by Joseph's refusal or enraged by the rejection, but he maintained his integrity even after all he had experienced. Whatever one may think about how his father favored him above his brothers, it has become apparent that Joseph has a character above reproach.

Although his vicissitudes were beyond drastic, the devastation did not change him. If there were any changes in Joseph, they were changes for the good. Any one of these unfortunate incidents would have brought many to their knees. How many could have endured his brothers' treacherous betrayal, having been left to die in a pit, then sold into slavery? From where did his strength come? As mentioned earlier, the Lord was with him. In the face of what must have been discouraging, disappointing, and depressing, his strength came from God, who appointed him for this journey. In essence, God was stretching the man for the dream. Lest we misread Joseph's man-made misfortunes, God was making a man through all of his troubles. Amid the darkness and despair, God was with him. How glorious is our God!

Joseph was arrested and put in prison. For the second time, through no fault of his own, he is betrayed and deprived of his place of privilege and position in his master's house, just as when his brothers stripped him of his coat of honor and standing in his father's house. After hearing from his wife the fabricated story, Potiphar did what most loving husbands would do; he "burned with anger" (Gen. 39:19). Just as with the hole, her false accusation seemingly destroyed the dream and dreamer.

There is no record of a criminal trial or trial attorney. Nor does the Bible tell us that Potiphar asked Joseph to defend the accusation against him or explain his side of the sorted and damning tale. His master simply "took him and put him in prison, the place where the king's prisoners were confined" (Gen. 39:20). Potiphar would have been well within his rights to execute Joseph. After all, his master, Potiphar, was "one of Pharaoh's officials, the captain of the guard" (Gen. 39:1).

However, Caralie suggests that perhaps Potiphar knew his wife and believed that she could fabricate such a lie.[2] One thing we know is that he trusted Joseph with everything he had. If he trusted Joseph to that degree, he had to have known that Joseph's character did not match such an accusation. If this story is difficult to hear, imagine how difficult it was to live.

For the second time, he is stripped of his coat, which undoubtedly distinguished him from the other servants and signified his position of authority. However, this time by Potiphar's wife, to use as evidence against him. The first time was to prove to his father his death, and this time it was to prove to his master his guilt. Neither of which was true. Still, without provocation, Joseph is repeatedly placed in unchartered territory and circumstances beyond his control.

Look at the dreamer now, falsely accused of attempted rape and locked away in prison. Of course, like people do today, many probably assumed his guilt solely based upon the accusation. Who would want to hear the dreams of a criminal? Who would even care that his dreams were of God? More importantly, how many would miss a move of God because of a lack of discernment? So often, we miss the message by erroneously judging the messenger.

Nevertheless, things are not always as they appear. Remember, absolutely nothing happens outside of God's authority, and He is in complete control no matter how things look, sound, or feel. Falsely accused and thrown into prison, but even in prison, God "showed him kindness and granted him favor in the eyes of the prison warden." In other words, "The Lord was with Him" (Gen. 39:21).

CHAPTER 3

From Potiphar's House to the Prison

Of course, as an enslaved person, Joseph was not in an ideal situation, to be sure. No one wants to be sold like property and enslaved. However, it is worth rehearsing that God was with him and gave him favor with his master. After rejecting Potiphar's wife, Joseph says to her, my master has left me in charge of everything and "does not concern himself with anything in the house; everything he owns he has entrusted to my care. No one is greater in this house than I am" (Gen. 39:8-9). There was an undeniable internal quality within Joseph larger than his external circumstances.

Indeed, nothing could mask, stifle, or snuff out the anointing of God upon his life. Whatever situation thrust upon him, nothing changed or altered what God put in him. God's anointing was upon him in the pit; he was still anointed in Potiphar's house, and as we shall discover, Joseph continued to be anointed in prison. Thus, there was more to Joseph than meets the eye. How many viable relationships have we missed by predetermining who and what a person is? How might our destiny be affected because we size a person up on the outside and never consider one's inner character and disposition?

I recently discovered some books I had stored over twenty years ago. Most of the books were dusty and brittle, and the pages had turned yellow. However, as I scanned through some of them, I found a wealth of knowledge by some of the most renowned Christian authors the world has ever known. Perhaps the old axiom is correct; judging a book by its cover is wrong. The full measure of a person is not her external qualities or weaknesses. Instead, to paraphrase the words of another prophetic dreamer, Martin Luther King Jr., the most significant part of one's being is her character.[1]

Calamity and adversity cannot dictate who you are. Our circumstances do not define us. Our outlook or perspective in any particular situation determines our outcome. Our attitude determines how we navigate life's adversities. Who you are and what God called you to be is not defined by anything other than what God has determined before the foundation of the world. He chose us; we did not choose Him (Eph. 1:4). It is in Him we live, move and breathe (Acts 17:28). God is our creator. Not only that, but He is our sustainer, and He "upholds all things by the word of His power" (Heb. 1:3). We are who and what God says we are, even in the face of undesirable situations and unfavorable circumstances.

Believers, what is in you is far more powerful than what is after you (1 Jn. 4:5). Life is fluid; situations and circumstances change day by day and sometimes moment by moment. However, "The reason the world does not know us" or understand what God is doing in us "is that it did not know Him." What holds true is that "now we are the children of God, and what we will be has not yet been known. But we know that when Christ appears, we shall be like Him, for we shall see Him as He is" (1 Jn. 3:1-2). For our God is truly great and greatly to be praised (Ps. 145:3).

Warren Wiersbe postulates, "Joseph lost his coat, but he kept his character."[2] His brothers stripped him of his coat, and Potiphar's wife snatched his cloak, but neither the coat nor cloak changed his anointing. It did not disrupt God's plans and purposes, and it changed absolutely nothing. It was in him. The enemy was after what was on him, but God was after what was in him. Thus, neither the assault by his brothers nor Potiphar's wife's assassination of his character altered anything. "From the days of John the Baptist until now, the kingdom of heaven has been subjected to violence" (or been forcefully advancing), "and violent people have been raiding it" (Mt. 11:12). Nevertheless, you cannot stop a move of God!

Just as in Potiphar's house, the supernatural power of God moved upon the warden of the prison. Consequently, "The warden put Joseph in charge of all those held in prison, and he was made responsible for all that was done there" (Gen. 39:22). Again, "the Lord was with Joseph and gave him success in whatever he did" (Gen. 39:23).

In prison, Joseph met Pharoah's "chief cupbearer and the chief baker," both of whom had been arrested by the king, for they angered the king (Gen. 40:2). The King James Version reads, "And Pharoah was wroth against" them. Whatever the case, they had fallen out of favor with the king, and it did not look promising for either of them. "The captain of the guard assigned them to Joseph, and he attended them" (Gen 40:4). Many would view this as a coincidence, but there are no coincidences in God, and He leaves nothing in life to luck or chance.

Thus, God does not leave us to play Russian roulette or the lottery with our lives. Such belief is Deism. Deists believe that God created the universe, then He stepped back, leaving man to figure it out on his own. Gary R. Habermas and Michael R. Licona submit that deists believe that "God exists and created the world but does not get involved in His creation."[3] Conversely, Erickson correctly notes, not only is God involved with His creation, but He is "actively at work within this world, influencing what takes place."[4]

As the attacks on his life intensified, so did the power and grace of God in Joseph's life. God stretched the gift within him beyond prophetic dreams. Now God gifted him to interpret dreams. All the time, God was making a man that He could use for His glory. To be sure, nothing about Joseph's life looked like God, but everything about his life was God. Sandra McCracken posits:

> So often, what we cannot see is the invisible hand of God at work in our lives. Our plans are not like his plans. As the hummingbird moves, his wings are invisible to us. So too, the work of God is often hard to see in the moment; nevertheless, something remarkable is happening.[5]

Hence, extraordinarily remarkable it was. Let us point out several noncoincidental facts. First, "the captain of the guard bought him from the Ishmaelites who had taken him" to Egypt (Gen. 39:1). Second, God gave him the favor to live in and rise to the head of the captain's household. Third, God blessed everything he did in that house to the point of unprecedented success and prosperity. Fourth, he was in "the place where the king's prisoners were confined" (Gen. 39:20). Fifth, God gave him favor with the warden and he was put "in charge of all those held in the prison, and he was made responsible for all that was done there" (Gen. 39:22).

Yes, it seems that there was an invisible force behind every adverse situation and circumstance in Joseph's life. It was God's mighty and providential hand at work to accomplish God's plans and purposes on the earth. That same hand is at work in our lives. God has not changed; His plans and objectives remain the same. The writer of Hebrews said, "The Lord is my helper; I will not be afraid. What can mere mortals do to me?" He is the same "yesterday, today, and forever"

(Heb. 13:6-8). So, yes, He is the same in character and nature, but God's plans are progressively unfolding.

Again, God supernaturally strategically placed him, without a trial, by the way, where he would have unfettered access to all the prisoners there. One must wonder why Potiphar did not put him "on trial or even execute him." As Wiersbe affirms, "Of course, God was in control, working out His wonderful plan."[6] Furthermore, do not forget Potiphar's substantial financial portfolio, which he attributed to Joseph. However, he had to take some action because his wife claimed attempted rape. He had to act.

Undoubtedly, they all knew the prisoner in charge. Prisoner in charge of the prison? Yes, the king's two men— the butler and the baker— knew him as he was assigned to serve them. They each had a dream which Joseph interpreted. For the butler, news that the king would restore him in three days was welcomed. However, the prophetic interpretation was terrible news for the baker. The baker was not so fortunate; the king would behead him in three days.

Here, Joseph must have seen a way out of this devastating predicament and explained to the butler, "I was forcibly carried off from the land of the Hebrews, and even here I have done nothing to deserve being put in a dungeon" (Gen. 40:15). This is the first time that we see any expression of emotion from Joseph. Caralie suggests that Joseph's unusual silence regarding what many would view as a normal response is "indicative of the state of shock following a traumatic event that renders a person mute and emotionally numb."[7]

Joseph does not ask for money, fame, any position of influence, or special privilege. He merely requested, "But when all goes well with you, remember me and show me kindness; mention me to Pharaoh and get me out of this prison" (Gen. 40:14). The only thing Joseph wanted was to be free.

The butler was locked up, not knowing when or if he would ever be free—what a simple request of a man who had no hope or expectation of ever being free again three days before his release. Not only that, but the king restored him to the same position as if nothing ever happened (Gen. 40:21). One would think that the butler would gratefully remember to mention Joseph to the king. "The chief cupbearer, however, did not remember Joseph; he forgot him" (Gen. 40:23).

It is sometimes difficult to grasp such ingratitude. Even more, how could the butler forget such an incredible gift of interpretation, which Joseph made clear, was of God? (Gen. 40:8). We often forget the people who bless our lives, and perhaps we take God's gifts for granted. However, we must never forget those whom God used to lift us from the pits of despair or those He used to speak life into us. They are gifts to the body of Christ "to equip His people for the works of service, so that the body of Christ may be built up" (Eph 4:12). Let us be very careful how we handle the blessings of God and not take God's gifts for granted.

The butler forgot Joseph for two years, which is a long time for him never to remember his supernatural experience with Joseph in prison. One must wonder if the butler consciously forgot Joseph or if God deliberately did not allow him to remember. Even if the butler was not spiritual, one must admit that what Joseph did was profound. Did it not run across his mind at least once? Remember, God has a plan and purpose for every life, and nothing happens without God's knowledge and consent. I am learning that God allows me to be wherever I am, and to face whatever I am facing; He permits it as well. Therefore, if God allows me to go through it, I must trust that He knows what is best for me even though I may not see or understand.

Joseph spent two more years in confinement for something he did not do. From all indications, prison is challenging, and undoubtedly it has to be difficult for someone who knows he is innocent.

CHAPTER 4

From the Prison to the Palace

Two years is a long time, but it must have seemed like a lifetime considering they were two years of imprisonment. Joseph had only one hope; that the butler would not forget him, which must have added to the frustration. Well, forget him; he did. Furthermore, how do you live with the thought of betrayal by your family? As if that was not enough, being falsely accused of a violent sexual crime? One led to a pit, then enslavement, and the other led to imprisonment with no trial, thus, no expected release date. Most would have given up by now—Depression atop all the disappointments and despair. How does one keep from losing his mind? Some turn to drugs, alcohol, other vices, or, sadly, even suicide. Others lose their faith and give up on God.

We may feel this way about Joseph because we think that we know how we would react. For the most part, all we can see and identify with is Joseph's pain and the negative occurrences in his life. However, what we cannot see is what God is doing inside him. Over and over again, the writer was gracious enough to bring us in on

Joseph's tedious journey as if we were the ones who needed comfort. He reminds us that through it all, the Lord was with Joseph.

Well, if you have ever been through any major crisis, one which you did not see a way out of, then you understand that that is everything! In a desperate or life-threatening dilemma, **the Lord with** you means all the difference in the world. When God is with you, He is more than the entire world against you (Rom. 8:31). In God's economy, God plus one is infinity!

I am not sure when Joseph overcame what must have been a sense of despondency spawned by repeated loss and defamation. There is no question that that would be a normal human response. However, there are signs that he did. What we do know is that through every crisis, Joseph rose above the fray. He met every adversity and every challenge with grace, and God allowed him to walk and thrive in that grace. The apostle Paul also experienced such supernatural grace. Because of the level of revelation given him, the level of anointing with which he walked, he was given "a thorn in his flesh, a messenger of Satan, to torment" him (2 Cor. 12:7).

Whatever the affliction, we do not know, but Paul prayed to God three times to relieve him of it. Nevertheless, God's response to Paul was, "My grace is sufficient for you, for my power is made perfect in weakness" (2 Cor. 12:8-9). Joseph, like Paul, must have had a special grace to endure all of these horrible experiences. However, things are about to turn around for him. God was still in complete control over every detail surrounding Joseph's life. God is sovereign, "for dominion belongs to the Lord, and He rules over the nations" (Ps. 22:28); He holds all things together (Col. 1:17) and "works out everything in conformity with the purpose of His will" (Eph. 1:11).

It is God who gives us the victory (1 Cor. 15:57). We do not fight for victory; therefore, the believer's victory over life's adversities is already won. Instead, our fight is one of celebration because of what God has done through Jesus Christ, our Lord. Paul explains it this way,

"No temptation has overtaken you except what is common to mankind." Moreover, "God is faithful; He will not let you be tempted beyond what you can bear. But when you are tempted, He will also provide a way out so that you can endure it" (1 Cor. 10:13).

The king had two dreams that troubled him to the point of weariness. "So he sent for all the magicians and wise men of Egypt. Pharaoh told them his dreams, but no one could interpret them for him" (Gen. 41:8). At last, the butler remembered his experience in prison and narrated the story to Pharoah. The Scripture tells us:

> Then the chief cupbearer said to Pharaoh, "Today, I am reminded of my shortcomings. Pharaoh was once angry with his servants, and he imprisoned me and the chief baker in the house of the captain of the guard. Each of us had a dream the same night, and each dream had a meaning of its own. Now a young Hebrew was there with us, a servant of the captain of the guard. We told him our dreams, and he interpreted them for us, giving each man the interpretation of his dream. And things turned out exactly as he interpreted them to us: I was restored to my position, and the other man was impaled." (Gen. 41:9-13)

Immediately the king sent for Joseph to interpret his disturbing dreams. Of course, if he was to stand before the king, he had to clean up to look presentable. Joseph met the king and listened to his dreams. He told the King just as he told the butler and the baker in prison, "I cannot" interpret dreams, "but God will give Pharaoh the answer he desires" (Gen. 41:16).

In Joseph, God was developing a man of character and integrity. The enemy tried to break him through all the tests, but God used those very trials to build him. He understood that whatever gift he possessed was from God and belonged to God. Everything belongs to God, "for whom and through whom everything exists" (Heb. 2:10), and "Every good and perfect gift is from above" (Jas. 1:17). Therefore, He knew to give God all the glory. We, too, must recognize that whatever potential credit, recognition, or fame may come our way because of unique gifts and talents, the glory must go to God.

He interpreted Pharoah's dreams as a warning from God. "God has revealed to Pharaoh what he is about to do" (Gen. 41:25). The prophetic word was seven years of plenty and "seven years of famine" (Gen. 41:26-27) "throughout the land of Egypt" (Gen. 41:29). Joseph also gave Pharoah a plan to administer the revelation properly. Hence, it was a spiritual word from God that would require spiritual implementation.

"Then Pharaoh said to Joseph, 'Since God has made all this known to you, there is no one so discerning and wise as you. You shall be in charge of my palace, and all my people are to submit to your orders. Only with respect to the throne will I be greater than you'" (Gen. 41:40). So impressed with Joseph even more, "the spirit of God" (Gen. 41:38), which he recognized in Joseph, the king put him "in charge of the whole land of Egypt" (Gen. 41:41).

The Scripture continues:

> Then Pharaoh took his signet ring from his finger and put it on Joseph's finger. He dressed him in robes of fine linen and put a gold chain around his neck. He had him ride in a chariot as his second-in-command, and people shouted before him, "Make way!" Thus he put him in charge of the whole land of Egypt. Then Pharaoh said to Joseph, "I am Pharaoh, but without your word, no one will lift hand or foot in all Egypt." (Gen. 41:42-44)

I know that his father's affirmation was incredibly significant to him, and it was probably the foundational act that helped develop his character. As mentioned earlier, Joseph knew who he was, and that level of confidence must have contributed to his steadfastness.

However, the king gave him his ring, a chain of gold, and a chauffeur-driven chariot. Ironically, he gave him a new coat, a new robe of distinction. This time it was, no doubt, another coat of many colors, and it was a robe fit for a king. How reminiscent.

There are two things to take away from this. First, Joseph was a prisoner accused of attempted rape. It was not just an anonymous woman in the community; it was the wife of the captain of the guard. Did anyone ever clear his name? Was he exonerated? The answer is no. There is no indication that Joseph's name was ever cleared. It was God who used the king to elevate Joseph. Hence, when it is God who advances and promotes, you do not need a name.

God knows how to establish you even when you do not have a so-called name. As we have seen in the life of Joseph, when God gets behind a bad name, He can still work miracles. In fact, God can do the same for a no-name. The truth is that even a person with a good reputation must have the backing and blessing of the Lord if a Kingdom work is to succeed.

Granted, the Bible indeed tells us to let our "light shine before others," but that is about His glory, not ours (Mt. 5:16). Also, "A good name is more desirable than great riches" (Prov. 22:1) and "better than fine perfume" (Ecc. 7:1), but that has to do more with one's own soul and benefit. I am always amazed when I hear about celebrity gospel music artists and so-called celebrity pastors talking about their "brand." They want to protect their "brand." What are celebrity gospel artists and celebrity Christian pastors anyway?

To be clear, they are protecting their brand for their benefit, not the kingdom of God. It is about maintaining their business standing and wealth, not advancing the kingdom and God's mission. In other words, they are building the kingdom of "me," not "the Kingdom of God." The kingdom of "me" needs your name, but the Kingdom of God already has a name. The Kingdom of God does not rest upon me and my reputation. Instead, it solely depends upon the precious finished work of

Jesus Christ our Lord. "But He was pierced for our transgressions, He was crushed for our iniquities; the punishment that brought us peace was on Him, and by His wounds, we are healed" (Isa. 53:5).

The reality is that any one of us is subject to fall, but God's Kingdom "cannot be shaken" (Heb. 12:28), "will never be destroyed," and "will stand forever" (Dan. 2:44). His "Kingdom is an everlasting Kingdom," and His "dominion endures through all generations" (Ps. 145:13). Moreover, there is but one name that matters in that Kingdom reality, and that is the name, Jesus.

Isaiah declares that Jesus Christ is the foundation in Zion, "a tried stone," "precious cornerstone," and a "sure foundation" (Isa. 28:16), which Paul reiterates in Romans 9:33, and a "sanctuary" to Israel, "a stone to strike and a rock to stumble" (Isa 8:14). "The stone which the builders rejected" who has become the chief cornerstone" (Ps. 118:22). Thus, "no one can lay any foundation other than the one already laid, which is Jesus Christ" (1 Cor. 3:11).

Peter identifies Jesus Christ as "a living stone" (1 Pet. 2:4). Jesus identifies Himself as "The stone the builders rejected" which has become the head of the corner (Mt. 21:42), as does the psalmist (Ps.118:22). John also reveals that Jesus was the temple of which He spoke that would be destroyed and in three days raised again (Mt. 2:18-21). Further, whoever falls upon the stone shall be saved, and those who do not will be crushed (Mt.21:44).

Therefore, it is "at the name of Jesus every knee should bow, in heaven and on earth and under the earth, and every tongue acknowledge that Jesus Christ is Lord, to the glory of God the Father" (Phil. 2:10-11). Christ has "supremacy. For God was pleased to have all His fullness dwell in Him, and through Him to reconcile to Himself all things" (Col. 1:18-20), and "Salvation is found in no one else, for there is no other name under heaven given to mankind by which we must be saved" (Acts 4:12). "All things were created for Him and by Him. He is before all things, and in Him, all things hold together" (Col.

1:16-17). Thus, "everyone who calls on" His name, not my name, "will be saved" (Rom. 10:13). There is but one name—at the end of the day— that actually matters.

Second, as Hendel explains, "It is a mistake to perceive Joseph as suddenly appointed to Egyptian viceroy after being in prison. Rather, Joseph had two senior appointments prior to his becoming viceroy of Egypt: master-slave in Potiphar's house (Gen. 39:2-5) as well as senior ward in the prison (Gen. 39:21-23)." Hence, "These appointments enriched him with necessary skills and leadership qualities."[1] Joseph did not stand before the king as a novice. He stood before the king after he had years of discipline and, no doubt, time with God, for the Lord was with him.

Every step of the way, God was with him. Through all of the ups and downs, the heartaches and disappointments, God was with him. Moreover, he was with God and honored God through it all. Our prayer should be, God, make me a man or woman of honor. Lord, teach me how to honor You.

God had an assignment for the man, but He had to prepare the man for the assignment. He practiced his gift first with his family. Then with the butler and the baker. Now he stands before the king, ready for God to use him and promote him to the position God wanted him to hold in the first place.

So it came to pass that Joseph's interpretation was correct. There were seven years of plenty and seven years of famine. However, Joseph had prepared all of Egypt to not only survive the famine, but they thrived. "There was famine in all the other lands, but in the whole land of Egypt there was food," so much so that "all the world came to Egypt to buy grain from Joseph because the famine was severe everywhere" (Gen: 41:53-57).

CHAPTER 5

The Miracle of Forgetfulness and Fruitfulness

Joseph had every reason, from a human perspective, to quit God, and candidly speaking, no one would blame him. However, he did not. As mentioned earlier, during the thirteen years of betrayal, false accusations, slavery, and imprisonment, Joseph met every challenge, rose to every occasion with a special grace, and found favor and success at every turn. He maintained his integrity and his faith in God. No matter the circumstance, his faith in God remained unwavering.

At thirty years of age and "second in command" (Gen. 41:43), Joseph is free to move throughout Egypt (Gen. 41:46), not as a king but just as if he was the king. In the words of Pharaoh, "without your word, no one will lift hand or foot in all Egypt" (Gen. 41:44). Pharaoh changed his name to "Zaphenath-Paneah and gave him Asenath, daughter of Potiphera, priest of On, to be his wife" (Gen. 41:45). They had two sons, Manasseh and Ephraim. "Joseph named his firstborn Manasseh and said, "It is because God has made me forget all my trouble and all my father's household" (Gen. 41:51).

By now, we should all agree that Joseph was a man of unassailable character; he was a man of God. We do not know precisely when Joseph was able to forget all the obvious pain that he lived. However, we know that it was the supernatural power of God that healed the hurt, pain, and disappointment in his heart. How else could Joseph make such a claim? Who else could have erased the memory of the excruciating suffering and humiliation? It was God. It was the supernatural power of God that rested upon Joseph's life that kept him at peace within himself.

He named his older son Manasseh after what God had done in his life. It was huge. Can you imagine having experienced the horrific things that Joseph experienced but without any memory of the pain? Joseph walked in a peace that surpassed all human comprehension (Phil.4:7). As mentioned earlier, the enemy was working on him, but God used every crisis to work a wonder in him. We, too, can experience the same measure of grace and contentment.

From the pulpit of the Metropolitan Tabernacle in 1878, Spurgeon proclaims, "some of my brothers and sisters here have not been walking near to God, and if so, their peace will not be perfect." However, he felt the need to turn his sermon into a prayer. He continues, "May you all know the text by experience. He who wrote it had felt it; may we who read it feel it too."[1] Similarly, John Piper concludes from Philippians 4:7 that we should "Ask the same Holy Spirit who inspired the writing to illumine the reading."[2]

Spurgeon and Piper speak of the perfect peace that only God can provide. God promised that He would keep us in "perfect peace, those whose minds are steadfast" or continually on Him (Isa. 26:3). "The fruit of that righteousness will be peace; its effect will be quietness and confidence forever" (Isa. 32:17). It is not a human peace; it is given supernaturally by God the Holy Spirit (Jn. 5:5; 14:27; Rom.

14:17). Paul prays, "May the God of hope fill you with all joy and peace" (Rom. 15:13), and "may the Lord of peace Himself give you peace at all times and in every way" (2 Thess. 3:16). My prayer for the reader is that this supernatural peace of God "be yours in abundance" (Jude 2), and like Joseph, that you walk near to God. The Lord was with him, and God is also with you.

Notice that the Scripture does not say that he forgot all that had happened to him, nor does it say that he forgot those who had wronged him by inflicting such evil upon him. However, it does infer that he did not remember the pain, stress, and agony it caused. In other words, Joseph did not suffer from the psychological distress, the emotional suffering, and the mental torment that would have otherwise destroyed his hope. God did not erase the memory of his loving father's covering or his evil brothers and their treachery. He did not erase the memory of Potiphar's wife's consequential lie and deception. Neither did he forget his time in prison.

The miracle is, God took away the anguish, hurt, pain, misery, and the enemy's intended consequence. God effectively removed any occasion for depression and discouragement, and as we will soon discover, there was no bitterness in his heart. The attacks upon his life and character did not distract Joseph from who he was and for whom he lived. He was not deterred, and the enemy's antics did not defer the dream. What the enemy employed to destroy him, God used to build him.

In effect, God used the enemy's attempted obstruction to construct a man of honor, integrity, and humility. The devil's aim is "to steal, kill and destroy," but God promises fullness of life when we align ourselves with His plans and purposes (Jn. 10:10). Thus, "God chose the foolish things of the world to shame the wise; God chose the weak things of the world to shame the strong" (1 Cor. 1:27).

Whatever God had planned for Joseph, he was on the enemy's radar, and the enemy knew that he had to stop this prophecy before it came to fruition. Thus, the enemy always goes after the dreamer to stop the dream. He always goes after the visionary to block the vision. That is why it is of the utmost importance that we keep our leaders, especially spiritual leaders, our visionaries, covered in prayer and any other area of temporal need.

Paul said, "If we have sown spiritual seed among you, is it too much if we reap a material harvest from you?" (1 Cor. 9:11). It is right to sow into those who bless your life and cover you and your family in prayer. After all, they feed and care for your soul (Heb. 13:17). However, all too often, church leaders suffer in silence and lack necessary temporal support. The body of Christ has lost far too many great leaders, men, and women, who were giants and generals in the Kingdom. Many have abandoned their post because of discouragement. Many suffer from depression, and others have walked away from the faith altogether.

Sometimes it is because of the insensitivity of those whom they serve, albeit unintentional. At other times it is because they fail to ask for help from those they love and serve. Several years ago, a very close friend and mighty woman of God encouraged me to share a particular personal crisis with my congregation that had driven me into a deep depression. In her tender yet persuasive voice, she pointed out to me that they loved me just as much as I loved them. She was correct. That was one of the most liberating words of encouragement I had ever received.

Equally, most leaders recognize that the vision is bigger than the visionary. For that reason, wise leaders are careful to surround themselves with those who can dream with them, then take the vision and run with it.

Joseph felt no grief from his troubles. None! Our great God took it away. Believers, I understand better the Scripture which says God will wipe away "every tear from their eyes" (Rev. 21:4). God "heals the brokenhearted, and He binds up their wounds" (Ps. 147:3).

There must be no pain if there are no tears, as tears usually accompany pain. Joseph felt no pain because his wounded heart was healed.

The second son he named Ephraim and said, "It is because God has made me fruitful in the land of my suffering" (Gen. 41:52). The psalmist declares, "What god is so great as our God? You are the God who performs miracles; You display Your power among the peoples" (Ps. 77:13-14). Only God can bring light out of darkness and order out of chaos, and He specializes in that which men deem impossible. "With God, all things are possible" (Mt. 19:26).

Although we sometimes fail to acknowledge it from our human perspective, and given our limited capacity, what about God is not miraculous? The air we breathe, the activity of our limbs, and the soundness of our minds are all supernaturally incomprehensible. The vast universe, the earth rotating on its axis, the sun's rising and setting, the moon hanging in its orbit, and the stars gleaming in their silvery sockets are unfathomable. In reality, everything about God is a miracle to us; He is a God of miracles, and everything about our existence is a supernatural of God phenomenon.

Thus, nothing shall be impossible to those who trust Him (Mk. 9:23) because nothing is too hard for God (Jer. 32:27). There is no plot or scheme against your life that God cannot handle. There is no lie told by the most professional prevaricator that God cannot overcome. Confinement in the most secure prison cannot prevent God from accomplishing His plans and purposes. Erickson posits, "There is no promise that persecution and suffering will not come, but rather that they will not prevail over us."[3] It is undeniable that weapons appeared to form in Joseph's life, and sometimes they seemed to sting, but ultimately, they could not, indeed, did not prosper.

Again, the most vital and consequential detail of Joseph's tragic misfortunes is that God was with him. Everything hinges upon God. For it is "in Him we live and move," and breathe (Acts 17:28). Yes, our very existence is because of God and His sustaining grace and mercy. He is in total control, and nothing happens in life outside the realm of God's authority, and no matter how things look, sound, or feel, He is in complete control.

Joseph was almost killed, betrayed, enslaved, falsely accused, and imprisoned, but at every turn, he found favor, prospered, and rose to greatness, notwithstanding his unfortunate dilemmas. Not only that but everywhere the afflictions led him, he blessed those with whom he came in contact. Potiphar was blessed; in prison, the butler was blessed, and in the palace, Pharaoh was blessed.

Look at the dreamer now. Fruit everywhere! Everywhere he went, and in everything he did, God caused prosperity for Joseph. By the way, anyone else connected to his life during this drama flourished. It is as if no scheme could stop him, no lie could destroy him, and no prison could hold him down. God was on a mission, and Joseph's life was in God's hands. Joseph never walked away from faith in God. Thus, he must have believed that God would work things out. Who would continue to walk with God without the hope that He would come through? There is no better combination: God's plan and your participation. Hence, he named his second son Ephraim because God faithfully caused him to prosper in the middle of his tempestuous storms.

Paul declares, "we are hard-pressed on every side, but not crushed; perplexed, but not in despair; persecuted, but not abandoned; struck down, but not destroyed" (2 Cor. 4:8-9). The Word of the Lord promises, "When you pass through the waters, I will be with you; and when you pass through the rivers, they will not sweep over you. When you walk through the fire, you will not be burned" (Isa. 43:2). It is God who fights our battles and rights all wrongs (Isa. 45:2). It is God who prepares a feast in our honor before the very presence of our enemies (Ps. 23:5).

From time to time, I remind my congregation that the only way you won't make it is if you quit. Joseph did not quit. Even during or after the many injustices, there is no indication that he desired to give up on God. At some point, he recognized that it was God all along (Gen. 45:7). "The Lord strong and mighty, the Lord mighty in battle" (Ps. 24:8). Why would anyone not serve a God like this?

Believers, never give up, and never throw in the towel. God has a plan, and His Word declares, "I Make known the end from the beginning, from ancient times, what is still to come. I say, My purpose will stand, and I will do that I please" (Isa. 46:10). It reminds me of the words of the Lord in the gospel of John after He preached to a crowd of five thousand. "When Jesus looked up and saw a great crowd coming toward Him, He said to Phillip, 'Where shall we buy bread for these people to eat?'" It was only a test of Phillip's faith because the writer goes on to declare that Jesus "already knew what He was going to do" (Jn. 6:5-6).

Whenever you are facing a crisis, trust that the Lord already has the answer, and He already knows what He is going to do. God knows where you are and the insurmountable mountains you face. In fact, He knows you by name (Ex. 33:17; Ps. 91:14; Isa. 43:1; Jn. 10:3), "the very hairs of your head are all numbered" (Lk.12:7), and "He knows the way that I take" (Job 23:10). "No temptation has overtaken you except what is common to mankind. And God is faithful; He will not let you be tempted beyond what you can bear. But when you are tempted, he will also provide a way out so that you can endure it" (1 Cor. 10:13).

CHAPTER 6

An Uncomfortable Reunion

Just as Joseph interpreted, there was a famine in Egypt and throughout the known world. Egypt was the one country prepared for such devastation, as only God can do. Therefore, "all the countries came to Egypt to buy grain" (Gen. 41:57). Who else did they have to stand before or bow, as the case might be? None other than Joseph, the once left for dead, enslaved, falsely accused, imprisoned man, turned governor. The entire world had to travel to Egypt for subsistence, not to see the king, but the man second to the king. Were it not for the grace and omniscience of God, the world, the human race, in that day, would have faced utter destruction.

When Jacob discovered that "there was grain in Egypt" (Gen. 42:1), he sent his sons, save Benjamin,[1] to trade for grain "so that we may live and not die" (Gen. 42:2) "for the famine was in the land of Canaan also" (Gen. 42:5). Upon their arrival, the first thing that happened was "they bowed down to him with their faces to the ground"

(Gen. 42:6). Some would view here that the prophetic dream had finally come true.

However, the prophetic dream was true and determined before the foundation of the world, and it was confirmed the day the young prophet released it into the atmosphere. That is why the Scripture teaches that we must walk by faith and not by what we see (2 Cor. 5:7). We live "on every word that comes from the mouth of God" (Mt. 4:4). Our faith should be in what God has said, not our circumstances. That we witness a thing come to pass is not what makes it true. What makes a thing true is that God said it in the first place. "God is not human, that He should lie, not a human being, that He should change His mind" (Num. 23:19). Hence, His Word is true (2 Sam. 7:28; Ps. 119:160; Jn. 17:17) and "It will not return empty but will accomplish what I desire and achieve the purpose for which I sent it" (Isa. 55:11).

It is apparent that they did not have an issue with bowing since when they arrived in Egypt, they did so without hesitation. We must then conclude that Joseph's brothers' problem was not only with the message; their problem was with the messenger. It was just as much the dreamer, if not more, than the dream itself which offended them. How many well-meaning people have missed God because of the vessel that God chose to use? How many have missed the message because of the messenger? They missed God because of the envy, ultimately hatred, towards God's set man in their hearts.

It is correct that the Scripture teaches, "It is better to take refuge in the Lord than to trust in humans" (Ps. 118:8). However, it is also important to remember that God uses people, and He sometimes speaks through the men and women whom He has chosen and appointed to carry His Word. Believers must walk close enough with God to discern the difference. God does not want us deceived by false teachers and preachers (1 Jn. 4:1), but He does call leaders and others to instruct us in the Lord (Mt. 28:19).

Their enmity towards Joseph impaired their vision, hearing, and cognitive ability to grasp and partake in what God was doing in the earth. In other words, as the adage goes, they could not see the forest for the trees. "Hatred paralyzes life; love releases it. Hatred confuses life; love harmonizes it. Hatred darkens life; love illuminates it."[2] They had done to their brother, not a stranger, the unimaginable. They entertained the thought of killing him, but they settled for selling him into slavery. We all probably know of siblings who struggle to get along; sibling rivalry is commonplace. However, most of us do not know of siblings, the likes of Joseph and his brothers. They hated him unto death.

On the other hand, Joseph did not share his brothers' hatred. Here, recall that the Scripture said they hated him because he was his father's favorite which, as D. F. Zeligs emphasizes, is "a fact which must have had a deep influence upon his character development and life experiences."[3] Further, "they hated him all the more" (Gen. 37:5) for his dream. Remarkably, the Scripture never suggests that Joseph had any disdain for them. In no place does the Scripture express or imply that he held any animosity towards his wicked brothers. God had put something uniquely special in him, and God guarded Joseph's heart. Of course, God had to have somewhere to set whatever it was that He put in him. It had to have somewhere to stick.

Thus, His heart was pure, and Joseph possessed the type of character and integrity that God could use. I often hear people proclaim, as if God is their witness, "God knows my heart," then I think to myself, "Exactly. That's the problem; God does know your heart." He "knows the secrets of the heart" (Ps. 44:21), and He knows "my thoughts before I think them" (Ps. 139:2).

When his brothers approached, like everyone else, they had to bow before the one who was in charge, Joseph. Clearly, God had prepared Joseph's heart for that day. It does not mean that he knew they were coming, although God may have revealed it to him. His

41

reaction was consistent with the character and integrity that he traversed all the other impossible situations thrust upon him. Here we witness such command under enormous pressure. Such a supernatural grace in which he walked.

His brothers did not recognize him, but he immediately knew them. However, "he pretended to be a stranger and spoke harshly to them (Gen. 42:7). How is it that they could not recognize him, but he had no difficulty recognizing them? First, according to their testimony, they assumed Joseph was dead by now (see Gen.42:13; 44:20). Furthermore, they knew that they had sold him into slavery. Many years had passed, and they would not have anticipated Joseph sitting in such a seat of authority. Although they knew that the Ishmaelites were headed to Egypt, the last place they would have expected to see Joseph was on the throne as "the governor of the land, the person who sold grain to all its people" (Gen 42:6).

Second, Joseph was not an Egyptian, but the king dressed him as if he were an Egyptian. Not just any Egyptian, but he was dressed like a king, a man of supreme authority commensurate to the power bestowed upon him. Also, wearing a beard was not a part of the Egyptian culture, especially among the elite. "He was clean-shaven," further, "he spoke to them in the Egyptian language through an interpreter."[4]

Third, Joseph had been through a lot, but he did not look like his troubles. The level of assault upon his life did not break him. God was with him, and God Kept him. Although an enslaved person, Joseph was the master-slave and lived in his master's house. Further, as a prisoner, he was the head trustee, de facto superintendent of the prison.

So, for whatever it is worth, even given his unfavorable circumstances, God exalted him to a place of prominence in both situations, which had to be a far cry from the ordinary enslaved people and prisoners. Remember, God always has to elevate a man to his calling and lift his consciousness to meet the assigned task.

The favor of God miraculously erased the pain of the injustices, and it also preserved or kept Joseph in a place of peace that only God could give. No wonder the psalmists said God does not "slumber nor sleep. The Lord watches over you, the Lord is your shade at your right hand" (Ps. 121:4-5). Not only that, but God's commitment is "to present you before his glorious presence without fault and with great joy" (Jude 1:24), chosen "in Him before the creation of the world." Why? "to be holy and blameless in His sight" (Eph. 1:4).

Joseph "spoke harshly to them" (Gen. 42:7), and some would argue he toyed with them. According to the Scripture:

> Joseph said to them, "It is just as I told you: You are spies! And this is how you will be tested: As surely as Pharaoh lives, you will not leave this place unless your youngest brother comes here. Send one of your number to get your brother; the rest of you will be kept in prison, so that your words may be tested to see if you are telling the truth. If you are not, then as surely as Pharaoh lives, you are spies!" And he put them all in custody for three days. On the third day, Joseph said to them, "Do this, and you will live, for I fear God: If you are honest men, let one of your brothers stay here in prison, while the rest of you go and take grain back for your starving households. But you must bring your youngest brother to me, so that your words may be verified and that you may not die." This they proceeded to do. (Gen. 42:14-20)

As most scholars and thinkers believe, that Joseph felt the need to test them does not mean that he sought revenge or payback. Most of us would agree that he had every human reason and right to do so, and he certainly had the power and the opportunity to exact retribution for their ungodly acts. They were, after all, responsible for the years of suffering that he had to endure. What was their present state of mind?

Had they repented? Had they learned anything from how they had mistreated him and his father? Perhaps this is what Joseph was after.

Matthew Henry submits that it was "not from a spirit of revenge, but to bring them to repentance."[5] Albert Barnes suggests that it "was to get at their hearts, to test their affection toward Benjamin, and to bring them to repent of their unkindness to himself."[6] Wiersbe posits, "His motivation was love, and his purpose was to bring them to repentance and reconciliation."[7] I argue that it was not merely Joseph's concern for his brothers' state of mind and hearts, but it was God's act of amazing grace leading them and calling them to Himself.

As a result, "This whole experience brought the ten men to the place where conviction was starting to germinate in their hearts."[8]

The Word says:

> They said to one another, "Surely we are being punished because of our brother. We saw how distressed he was when he pleaded with us for his life, but we would not listen; that's why this distress has come on us." Reuben replied, "Didn't I tell you not to sin against the boy? But you wouldn't listen! Now we must give an accounting for his blood." They did not realize that Joseph could understand them since he was using an interpreter. (Gen. 42:21-23)

After many years of covering their sin, their "sin found them out" (Num. 32:23). Numbers 32:23 is often used as an emotional weapon by those who believe they have been wronged. Or by self-righteous people who seek to judge others while not considering their own unrighteousness. What believers sometimes forget or choose to ignore is that "all have sinned and fall short of the glory of God" (Rom. 3:23). Moreover, "We all, like sheep, have gone astray, each of us has turned to our own way" (Isa. 53:6a). In other words, "There is no one righteous, not even one" (Rom. 3:10), but thank God that "the LORD has laid on him the iniquity of us all" (Isa 53:6b).

Such a worldly, thus shallow interpretation is incorrect. It does not mean that God will expose your sins and weaknesses to the world. Besides, such street revenge is beneath God's character. Conversely, He does not want or need to operate on the human playing field of revenge. That is just not who our God is. God wants to heal sin-sickness, not embarrass the sinner. "The Lord is not slow in keeping his promise, as some understand slowness. Instead, He is patient with you, not wanting anyone to perish, but everyone to come to repentance" (2 Pet. 3:9). Rather than exposure to the world, the passage means that your sins will catch up with your consciousness, and so it did.

The world did not know what they had done, but what had been thrust upon them awakened everything in them. They assumed that God was punishing them for what they had done to Joseph some twenty years earlier out of a guilty conscience. It is reminiscent of Peter, who, after denying Jesus, was quickened by the rooster crowing as Jesus promised (Mt. 26:75). In every life, the rooster will crow.

However, it was God who was at work lovingly bringing these men to a place of repentance. And that is the exact manner in which our longsuffering, full of compassion, "abounding in love and faithfulness" (Ps. 86:15), Father draws us all. He draws us by His Holy Spirit to Himself (Jn. 6:44). It is with love, "an everlasting love" that God has "drawn" us "with unfailing kindness" (Jer. 31:3), demonstrated in the fact that "While we were still sinners, Christ died for us" (Rom. 5:8).

The Scripture tells us:

> He turned away from them and began to weep but then came back and spoke to them again. He had Simeon taken from them and bound before their eyes. Joseph gave orders to fill their bags with grain, to put each man's silver back in his sack, and to give them provisions for their journey. After this was done for them, they loaded their grain on their donkeys and left. (Gen. 42:24-25)

Notice three things to dispel further the notion that Joseph was acting maliciously. First, after he heard his brothers, particularly Reuben, who, in no uncertain terms, gave them the infamous "I told you so" diatribe, Joseph turned his face away so that they could not see him weep. They were not the tears of a man with malicious intent. Although Joseph was not a perfect man, he was a man whose life was thrust into calamity after calamity. Yet, throughout this drama, we see Joseph use what was meant to destroy him, only to drive him into his destiny.

Second, although Joseph sold them grain, he gave back every dime they used to buy it. Why would a man with ill intentions return anything of value, especially when he did not have to? That Joseph refused their money is a clear indication that he did not harbor any animosity. Third, he gave them provisions for the long trip home. Is it not unusual for an enemy to feed his enemies or even care that they have food, fresh drinking water, and other supplies necessary for the journey?

Joseph was not merely a good man; he was a God-man. God was with Joseph, and he was a man of impeccable character. So, when we see how he maintained his integrity from the pit, Potiphar's house, the prison, to the palace, it is not simply because he is a decent or good man. Rob Starner aptly notes, "It's forgiveness he chooses, and vengeance he refuses."[9]

CHAPTER 7

The Ultimate Test

At the place where they stopped for the night, one of them opened his sack to get feed for his donkey, and he saw his silver in the mouth of his sack. "My silver has been returned," he said to his brothers. "Here it is in my sack." Their hearts sank, and they turned to each other, trembling, and said, "What is this that God has done to us?" (Gen. 42:27-28)

Conviction is setting in. We saw God at work in and through Joseph, and now we see God at work in his brothers. Although before this reunion, their behavior and character were more than questionable. However, we see that no one is outside the reach of God, the Holy Spirit. God used Joseph's compassion to arrest them. Hence, their query is, are we being judged or punished by God?

We should never give up, even on the most immoral or wicked among us. Even more, we should never underestimate the power of God to touch whom He will. Remember, people, all people, belong to God, and no one is outside of God's reach. It is not God's will that anyone should be lost. He cares for every living soul, "not wanting anyone to perish, but everyone to come to repentance" (2 Pet.3:9). A line from Ira Stanphill's hymn reminds us that "Tho millions have come, there's still room for one. There is room at the cross for you."[1]

The Word of the Lord says:

> "Then the man who is lord over the land said to us, 'This is how I will know whether you are honest men: Leave one of your brothers here with me and take food for your starving households and go. But bring your youngest brother to me, so I will know that you are not spies but honest men. Then I will give your brother back to you, and you can trade in the land.'" (Gen. 42:33-34)

When the nine brothers returned to Canaan, they rehearsed all that happened in Egypt with their father. Unquestionably, they were hard-pressed to inform Jacob that they had to leave Simeon as a hostage, but the most difficult part was that they had to return to Egypt with Benjamin as ransom. Otherwise, they would never speak to the governor, buy the desperately needed grain they needed to survive, or see Simeon again. In essence, they were in an untenable predicament. They left pressure in Egypt, but they faced even more pressure before their father in Canaan.

Initially, Jacob understandably refused, saying, "My son will not go down there with you; his brother is dead, and he is the only one left. If harm comes to him on the journey you are taking, you will bring my gray head down to the grave in sorrow" (Gen. 42:38). Who could blame him for his apprehension? He lost Joseph over twenty years ago, and now Simeon is gone. How could he possibly risk losing Benjamin, his beloved Rachael's other son? Just the thought was more than he could bear.

Again, we see that Jacob, though he could not prove it, suspected that they were responsible for Joseph's demise some twenty years prior.[2] Later, however, Jacob acquiesced:

> Then their father Israel said to them, "If it must be, then do this: Put some of the best products of the land in your bags and take them down to the man as a gift—a little balm and a little honey, some spices and myrrh, some pistachio nuts and almonds. Take double the amount of silver with you, for you must return the silver that was put back into the mouths of your sacks. Perhaps it was a mistake. Take your brother also and go back to the man at once. And may God Almighty grant you mercy before the man so that he will let your other brother and Benjamin come back with you. As for me, if I am bereaved, I am bereaved." (Gen. 43:11-14)

For obvious reasons, Jacob reluctantly accepted what he believed was sure to be a disaster in the making.

When they returned to Egypt, they came with Benjamin and stood before Joseph. Still not recognizing him, Joseph had his servants prepare a sumptuous feast at his house for his brothers, where Simeon joined them. "Deeply moved at the sight" of Benjamin, Joseph abruptly ran from their presence to look "for a place to weep. He went into his private room and wept there" (Gen. 43:30). What a relief this must have been for Joseph. No harm had come to Benjamin, his only whole brother, by the hands of his evil and envious brothers. Hence, their word was true.

Still, Joseph needed to know if they had matured in character; he needed to see their hearts. Therefore, he instructed his "steward" to "Fill the men's sacks with as much food as they can carry and put each man's silver in the mouth of his sack" (Gen. 44:1). Not only that, but he further directed him to "put my cup, the silver one, in the mouth of the youngest one's sack, along with the silver for his grain" (Gen.

44:2). Spiritually, God was still at work in them, going after their hearts.

It appears that they kept their promise to the governor, which relieved them of that pressure. Now they would travel back to meet their father in Canaan with more good news, assuaging them of that pressure. In their minds, all is well and ends well. They left Egypt with the grain, Simeon and Benjamin, and their father would be pleased. Thus, alleviating him of the fear of losing Simeon and Benjamin. However, having traveled a short distance, Joseph sent his steward to find them and accuse them of stealing Joseph's silver cup. This he did.

Nevertheless, they had done everything required of them. They were so confident of their innocence that they volunteered, "If any of your servants is found to have it, he will die; and the rest of us will become my lord's slaves" (Gen. 44:9). When the steward searched their belongings, the silver cup was found in Benjamin's possession. "At this, they tore their clothes. Then they all loaded their donkeys and returned to the city" (Gen. 44:13). "The thought of losing" Jacob's youngest son, Benjamin, "and consequently not fulfilling the promise they made to their father incited their rending of clothes."[3] Naturally, they were baffled and perplexed. Even more, they were distraught.

Given the circumstances, Benjamin had to die, and the others were to end up in the same state that they left Joseph; they would be enslaved in Egypt. At this point, for whatever it was worth, they were profoundly disturbed and full of sorrow.

Five times they had to bow before Joseph. The first time the ten brothers "bowed down to him with their faces to the ground" (Gen. 42:6). The second time, they "presented themselves to Joseph" (Gen. 43:15), with Benjamin with them. The third time was when Joseph met them at his house for dinner (Gen. 43:26), and the fourth time they bowed again even lower (Gen. 43:28). However, the fifth time, they not only bowed but "they threw themselves to the ground before him" (Gen. 44:14) because of their fear of losing Benjamin. Brokenness will make you forget protocol, formalities, dignity, and pride. They are almost ready. There truly is beauty in brokenness.

Judah even spoke up in what seemed to be a genuine sense of love and concern for his father. He makes a heart-wrenching, impassioned plea for the release of Benjamin in exchange for his own life. "Now then, please let your servant remain here as my lord's slave in place of the boy and let the boy return with his brothers" (Gen. 44:33). Judah continues, "How can I go back to my father if the boy is not with me? No! Do not let me see the misery that would come on my father" (Gen. 44:34). Perhaps Joseph's brothers are now ready for the next move in God's mission.

They had to be tested or proven because, as we shall see, God was after them as much as He was after Joseph. They were all to be used by God to fulfill His mission. "When they implore his forgiveness as men praying to God, he responds not as a king, but as a source of sustenance and comfort."[4]

Joseph's dream is coming to pass, God is moving in their hearts, and God's plans and purposes are being fulfilled. No matter how grim things appear, God's will, His plans, and His purposes will come to pass. Nothing happens outside God's providential care, and He is always in complete control. If they were to be used on mission with God, He needed them to have "a broken and contrite heart," as David was aware, "God will not despise" (Ps. 51:17). God has never used anyone in the Bible, or today for that matter, who was not first and foremost broken, and whose feet were not feet of clay.

CHAPTER 8

God Uses Brokenness

Joseph revealed himself to his brothers when he could no longer contain himself. He dismissed his servants and "wept so loudly that the Egyptians heard him, and Pharaoh's household heard about it" (Gen. 45:2). His brothers were so "terrified at his presence" (Gen.45:3) that they could not speak. Joseph assured them that they had no reason to fear. He not only forgave them, but he comforted them and relieved them of their guilt, saying, "do not be angry with yourselves for selling me here, because it was to save lives that God sent me ahead of you" (Gen. 45:5).

It was bigger than the once seventeen-year-old Joseph. Thus, it required a mature, tried-by-fire God-man to love and forgive to that degree. It is without a doubt that Joseph had weathered the storms of life, and he had the capacity to walk in such grace. Under the same or similar trials, many would have walked away from God and renounced any calling they think they may have heard. He had to see beyond himself, and he had to see through the eyes of God. More importantly, Joseph knew that "God had divinely planned and allowed him to suffer."[1]

As Christians, we are to take on the mind of Christ (Phil. 2:5) so that we may, by faith, navigate life's challenges. Our minds are to be renewed so that we may see clearly what the will of the Lord is for our lives (Rom. 12:2). God does not want us to succumb to the "devil's schemes." Instead, we are to stand and "be strong in the Lord" (Eph. 6:10-11) and pray that "the eyes of our understanding may be enlightened in order that we may know the hope to which He has called" (Eph. 1:18).

However arrogant or braggadocious he may have been at age seventeen, Joseph was now broken. God had raised Joseph to the level of his calling and anointing. God had elevated him to meet the holy hour, the God-assigned task for His plans and purposes. Everything God needed to work out of Joseph in order to work in and through Joseph, God had accomplished. He was settled, focused, and ready to do God's will in the earth. Likewise, the Word of the Lord promises the believer: "And the God of all grace, who called you to his eternal glory in Christ, after you have suffered a little while, will himself restore you and make you strong, firm, and steadfast" (1 Pet. 5:10).

As mentioned earlier, the dream or vision is always bigger than the dreamer or visionary. What God has placed in you is greater than you and whatever issues you may face. God was after what was in Joseph, God was after what was in his brothers, and He got exactly what He wanted. Joseph was broken. He was able to rule another man's kingdom because he had been broken. Joseph was a stranger, and had he sensed any spirit other than humility in him, the king would never have entrusted to Joseph his kingdom.

If arrogance and pride existed, they dissipated between the pit and prison. God never uses a man or woman who has not been broken.

Joseph knew God from the beginning, and if there was any in him, for sure, he now knew God without pride and egotism. He knew God through humility born out of humiliation. The psalmist said God "sent a man before them— Joseph, sold as a slave" (Ps. 105:17). Yes, you read that correctly. God sent him. He did not send him in a glorious parade. God did not send him the scenic route. He did not send him to Egypt in a private jet or by a first-class ticket. Joseph's journey to the palace was no flowery bed of ease. It was a tedious journey mired with treachery. It was a riddled journey of brokenness.

God was breaking a man to make a mature man throughout the process. Based on his testimony, one must wonder when Joseph precisely felt sent. At what point did he realize he was anointed to suffer? When did his troubled and turbulent path become well with his soul? Was it in the pit? Potiphar's house? Prison? Who knows? However, by the time he reached the palace, there was no question that the brokenness made Joseph a better man rather than a bitter man. As we view his actions and listen to his testimony, it becomes clear that it really was well with his soul.

Similarly, Joseph's brothers were broken after having met him. His brothers knew the blessings of God but not the burden. They knew God from their father's experience, but like Joseph, they now find God through their own. Joseph's test or exercise literally put the fear of God in them. Even more than a genuine sense of love and concern for their father, as mentioned in the previous chapter, there must have been tremendous fear.

Their hatred for Joseph and selfish pride once rendered them void of any true honor or empathy for their father. In a sense, one can safely assume that they were just as much in bondage as Joseph. Their blindness and heartlessness robbed them of their humanity and any sense of decency. The hands of those who inflicted Joseph's pain were the very hands responsible for their self-imposed imprisonment of guilt. We hear the agony in Judah's speech. Judah posits:

"So now, if the boy is not with us when I go back to your servant, my father, and if my father, whose life is closely bound up with the boy's life, sees that the boy isn't there, he will die. Your servants will bring the gray head of our father down to the grave in sorrow. Your servant guaranteed the boy's safety to my father. I said, 'If I do not bring him back to you, I will bear the blame before you, my father, all my life!' "Now then, please let your servant remain here as my lord's slave in place of the boy, and let the boy return with his brothers. How can I go back to my father if the boy is not with me? No! Do not let me see the misery that would come on my father." (Gen. 44:30-34)

Day in and day out, they watched their father slowly die from grief over the loss of Joseph. Apparently still grieving Joseph's loss, the potential loss of Benjamin would be the final death knell signifying the end of his mourning. The grief must have turned Jacob into a shell of the man he once was. I have witnessed grief change the very nature of people. It had to be profound emotional pain. Remember, he loved Joseph so much that his extreme love alienated his other sons to the point that they were willing to kill Joseph or at least entertain the idea. There is no doubt that Jacob's grief negatively affected him and everyone around him.

Through the many years of covering their guilt yet carrying the responsibility of having disposed of Joseph, or so they thought, we finally see that they have a conscience. There is no doubt that they lived with and experienced conviction from time to time. Remember, the rooster is always crowing in our lives. However, this experience was the straw that broke the camel's back, so to speak, and brought them to a place of brokenness, true repentance. No one is outside the reach of God. In other words, nothing and no one is impervious to God's Word, His way, and His will (Heb. 4:13).

To his father, Judah offered to "bear the blame" for the rest of his life if anything happened to Benjamin, and he offered to exchange his life for the boy's life with the governor. His speech and actions are a true sign of brokenness, thus, repentance. It is never enough to only utter the words, "I'm sorry." Often they are empty words unless one learns how to "be sorry." One is not truly sorry without restoring the breach, repairing the damage, or replacing the loss they have caused. Judah was willing to go the distance to make their egregious deeds right. He was prepared to make it right, whether at Canaan with his father, or with Joseph, the governor, in Egypt. A sorrowful heart takes full responsibility and bears the necessary burden of restitution. This time, Judah hit the right note.

Only God could bring all of these events into play. We see God's providential hand of mercy and grace from the pit to the palace at work. Charles Swindoll maintains that although God's will, His plans, may indeed be a mystery to us, "the world," nonetheless, "is not out of control, spinning wildly through space. Nor are earth's inhabitants at the mercy of some blind, random fate." Thus, "When God created the world and set the stars in space, He also established the course of this world and His plan for humanity."[2]

So yes, God can and does use brokenness. He can use whatever He chooses to accomplish His will with His creation. After all, this is His world, the earth, and everything that dwells therein (Ps. 24:1). Absolutely nothing happens outside of His authority, and no matter how it looks, He is in complete control. God can use anything and anyone to accomplish His will, and nothing can thwart the plans and purposes of God.

The apostle Paul says, "We are troubled on every side, yet not distressed; we are perplexed, but not in despair; persecuted, but not forsaken; cast down, but not destroyed" (2 Cor. 4:8-9). If God allows us to be broken, it is not to destroy us, but to bring us to a place of greater faith, trust, and in due course, total dependence upon the Lord.

It is through the process, or shall I say, the ministry of brokenness, we learn to surrender our will to His. That is when we are able to say it and mean it; it is indeed well with my soul.

Now we see the Lord's longsuffering (2 Pet. 3:9) and loving-kindness, which is "better than life" (Ps. 63:3), at work through brokenness. In the life of Joseph and even his brothers, through His wise providence, God used brokenness, and it really was God all the time. There is beauty in brokenness when God is in it, after all. Never forget. Our God is sovereign and in full control over people, places, and things.

CHAPTER 9

It Was God All the Time

That God causes all things to work together for our good speaks to the providential hand of God. Although the Bible does not expressly use the word providence, it most certainly intimates that God's providential hand is active in human affairs. The Word says:

Then Joseph said to his brothers, "Come close to me." When they had done so, he said, "I am your brother Joseph, the one you sold into Egypt! And now, do not be distressed and do not be angry with yourselves for selling me here because it was to save lives that God sent me ahead of you. For two years now, there has been famine in the land, and for the next five years, there will be no plowing and reaping. But God sent me ahead of you to preserve for you a remnant on earth and to save your lives by a great deliverance. "So then, it was not you who sent me here, but God. He made me father to Pharaoh, lord of his entire household, and ruler of all Egypt. (Gen. 45:4-8)

Joseph revealed to them that it was God all the time. Some theologians and scholars suggest that it was not as simple as his brothers sold him as a slave to Egypt; God sent him. They may have sold him into slavery, but it was God who sent him to Egypt. In other words, the enemy may have started it, but it was as if God snatched it, owned it, and used it for His glory. I cannot here recount the many occasions I knew that an attack originated from the enemy. However, God stepped in as if He had initiated it and owned it. God used and turned around in my favor every trial, storm, dark day, and loss.

No wonder Oswald Chambers posits it is God who ordains "the circumstances of a saint's life."[1] Wiersbe agrees that "God is in control of circumstances."[2] Stephen Campbell suggests that God allows His people to go through difficulties and that "sometimes God may even orchestrate these trials." He further notes that "God allowed his own son to experience intense trials in the Garden of Gethsemane."[3] Chambers adds, "All your circumstances are in the hand of God, and therefore, you don't ever have to think they are unnatural or unique."[4] The psalmist proclaims that the whole of my life, every second of my destiny, is only in the hand of God (Ps. 31:15). To this Psalm, Spurgeon comments, David "had no fear as to his circumstances, since all things were in the divine hand."[5]

Perhaps that is why Romans 8:28 makes all the sense in the world and encourages our faith: "And we know that in all things God works for the good of those who love Him, who have been called according to His purpose" (Rom. 8:28). Chambers goes on to suggest that it is a matter of "our unfaithfulness" to God that we do not or cannot recognize that He "ordained the situation."[6]

Another problem for some believers is that they interpret this verse to mean "some things," not "all things," work out for our good. Or only the "good things" work out for our good. However, the Word of the Lord is explicitly clear, "All things," not some things or merely the good things. All means all. God has a way that is beyond human comprehension, and "He performs wonders that cannot be fathomed, miracles that cannot be counted" (Job 5:9). Only the Spirit knows the depths of God (1 Cor. 2:10-11).

Hence, the awesomeness of our God is incomprehensible. He is a transcendent God. According to Millard Erickson, "Correlated with God's transcendence is human finiteness." As such, "He goes beyond our categories of understanding." He "can never be grasped within our finite concepts or by our human vocabulary."[7] At the same time, our transcendent God is knowable or immanent. "God is immanent in the lives of His people who repent of their sins and live by faith to accomplish the goals of His redemptive grace."[8] Thus, we can relate to the God we serve as we are being transformed into His image.

For the Christian faith, "the basis of authority for knowing reality (God) is the Bible," which is, in essence, "God's written revelation to humanity."[9] God is a self-revealing God, and "the Biblical pronouncement on the existence of God, and all else, is self-attesting or self-authenticating."[10]

Moreover, Paul writes, "since what may be known about God is plain to them because God has made it plain to them. For since the creation of the world God's invisible qualities—his eternal power and divine nature—have been clearly seen, being understood from what has been made, so that people are without excuse" (Rom. 1:19-20). Royce Gordon Gruenler rightly notes: "The signature of God is upon everything He has made and reflects His authorship." As well, all of humanity "has an awareness of God's glory and moral perfection." As such, the law of God is innate, deeply rooted "in the human heart and is perceived morally."[11]

However you assess the sorted story of Joseph's journey, it is much better to be in the hand of God than the hands of the enemy. Or, as Wiersbe mentions of Abraham's wrong choice, it is "safer in a famine in His will than in a palace out of His will"[12] (see also Genesis 12). Nevertheless, God chose the path Joseph took, not the devil. His brothers pushed him into a pit and sold him into slavery, but Joseph was never in their hands. He was a slave in Potiphar's house and falsely accused by Mrs. Potiphar of a dastardly crime, but he was never in their hands. He was locked in a prison, but he was never in the hands of the warden. Joseph was always in the hand of God. For the Lord was with him, blessed him, and elevated him above the fray (Gen. 39:2-4, 21-23).

Believers are never in the hands of the devil, whatever the situation or circumstance. The enemy may orchestrate events, but he cannot determine our destiny. Like Joseph, we too are in the hand of God, and Jesus promises, "no one will snatch them out of my hand" (Jn. 10:28). Putting it succinctly, the enemy does not set God's agenda.

From time to time, we have all been guilty of rebuking the path or circumstances, believing that it is of the devil when it is, in fact, God. It is out of our finitude that makes Joseph's troubles seem an unlikely act of God. One reason, as Swindoll asserts, is that most believers only have a "horizontal perspective" of life's challenges. Thus, "We lack the vertical view."[13]

I submit that whenever we fight that which we can see and feel, the battle is already lost. During spiritual warfare, the biblical Christian's vantage point is to look at what is behind what we think we see and feel. In other words, our fight is not against that which is flesh; it is against that which is spirit, or that which cannot be seen, as attested by Paul in Ephesians 6.

Furthermore, probably because of the pervasive heresy or "pernicious theology"[14] taught today, it is challenging to acknowledge this was all by the hand of God. The psalmist is correct; God sent a man, "even Joseph" (Ps. 105:17 KJV), not the devil. Of course, it was not the path we would have chosen, but it was the path that God chose for Joseph. Like it or not, or whether we can comprehend it, God did this thing.

Although we readily embrace the will of God, the plan of God, we often struggle with the path. We pray, then celebrate the promises, but the path is rarely acceptable. Many lose heart during what I call "the in-between." It is the process that causes frustration and sometimes doubt and fear. Some faint between the promise and the manifestation. Waiting on God through a storm is usually the most challenging time in a believer's walk.

Listen to Job's encouragement: "But he knows the way that I take; when he has tested me, I will come forth as gold" (Job 23:10). Our Creator knows us by name (Isa. 43:1). He knows where we are and is concerned for every minute detail of our lives. Absolutely nothing happens outside of His authority; no matter how it looks, He is in complete control. Again, God sent a man, not the devil.

God can use anything and anyone to accomplish His will, and nothing can thwart the plans and purposes of God. Even if the circumstances may seem messy or in disarray, we must know that "God's plan is not frustrated," nor does He alter His plan because of it. "He is not sitting on the edge of heaven," head in hands, "wondering what will happen next."[15] Our sovereign God does all things well (Mk. 7:37), He does it His way, and He does it according to His will and good pleasure (Phil. 2:13).

There is no better witness to the sovereign hand of God in this story than Joseph. He confirmed, himself, that it was God. Either he was completely insane, in serious denial, or thoroughly convinced. Because he functioned, exercised discretion, and maintained his integrity throughout the ordeal despite his abnormal circumstances, I trust that he was thoroughly persuaded and honestly believed that it was God. He could not walk in that level of love and grace without solid faith in God.

He declared: "And now, do not be distressed and do not be angry with yourselves for selling me here, because it was to save lives that God sent me ahead of you" (Gen. 45:5). Again, he asserted: "But

God sent me ahead of you to preserve for you a remnant on earth and to save your lives by a great deliverance. So then, it was not you who sent me here, but God. He made me father to Pharaoh, lord of his entire household and ruler of all Egypt" (Gen. 45:7-8).

Although Joseph is a prominent actor in this story, God is the star and leading character. God was sovereign over the pit, Potiphar's house, the prison, and the palace. His sovereignty "expresses the very nature of God as all-powerful and omnipotent, able to accomplish His good pleasure, carry out His decreed will, and keep His promises."[16] God is still sovereign, and He continues to rule and super rule over life and the affairs of humankind.

God had a plan from the beginning of time, and His intents and purposes unfold progressively throughout human history. Our sovereign God works His plans, carries out His purposes, and keeps His promises. He is a promise keeper!

CHAPTER 10

God the Promise Keeper

The Word of the Lord says, "The Lord is not slow in keeping his promise" (2 Pet. 3:9). In his benediction to the church at Thessalonica, Paul prays, "May God Himself, the God of peace, sanctify you through and through. May your whole spirit, soul, and body be kept blameless at the coming of our Lord Jesus Christ. The One who calls you is faithful, and He will do it" (1 Thess. 5:23-24). The psalmist affirms, "Your word, LORD, is eternal; it stands firm in the heavens. Your faithfulness continues through all generations; You established the earth, and it endures" (Ps. 119:89-90). "Know therefore that the LORD your God is God; He is the faithful God, keeping His covenant of love to a thousand generations of those who love Him and keep His commandments" (Deut. 7:9).

The Scripture is replete not only with the promises of God but with many examples and testimonies of His faithfulness. God is a promise keeper! He is not slack but faithful and firm concerning that which He has promised (2 Pet. 3:9). "For no word from God will ever fail" (Lk. 1:37). Jesus declared, "Heaven and earth will pass away, but my words will never pass away" (Mt. 24:35). Not only does He keep His Word, but God watches over His Word to ensure that it is fulfilled (Jer. 1:12). Hence, the Lord promises that whatever He releases from His mouth "will not return empty, but will accomplish what I desire and achieve the purpose for which I sent it" (Isa. 55:11). R. A. Torrey asserts, "God's faithfulness is manifested in His keeping His promises and covenant to the very letter, in His fulfilling every word that goes out of His mouth, regardless of what man does."[1]

I have often heard my good friend, brother, and mentor, Jimmy Sneed, pastor of Rivers of Living Water Church, Albany, Georgia, teach that whenever God makes a covenant, He knows from the beginning that it would be up to Him to hold up both ends. We refer here to a unilateral rather than a bilateral covenant. Only one party has to perform.

In essence, God's promises are just that. They are His promises, and God's promises do not depend upon human beings' faithfulness or limited abilities. For instance, the Scripture teaches that if we confess "Jesus is Lord" and believe in our hearts that "God raised him from the dead," we "will be saved" (Rom. 10:9). However, Jesus makes it clear, "No one can come to me unless the Father who sent me draws them" (Jn. 6:44).

The point here is that God draws us to Himself by His Holy Spirit; we do not come to God independently. Then, He saves us, but only after He calls us to salvation. Hence, God holds up both ends of His covenant. He draws, calls, saves, and keeps us. There is nothing within us humans that remotely resembles righteousness and faithfulness. The truth is that human beings never tire of sin. We may get tired from sinning, but not of sin. Even Paul says, "For in my inner being I delight in God's law; but I see another law at work in me, waging war against the law of my mind and making me a prisoner of the law of sin at work within me" (Rom. 7:22-23).

Our only hope is that we are delivered by Jesus Christ and Him alone, "Thanks be to God" (Rom. 7:25). If we are complete, it is because we are complete in Him (Col.2:10). If we are righteous, it is because we are covered in His righteousness. Isaiah declares, "For He has clothed me with the garments of salvation, He has covered me with the robe of righteousness" (Isa. 61:10). Paul says, "God made Him who had no sin to be sin for us so that in Him we might become the righteousness of God" (2 Cor. 5:21). In any other form, it is called self-righteousness.

The spiritual reality is that the saintliest among us, or as they say in the Pentecostal tradition, those who are "truly saved and sanctified" are not holy because of anything they have done other than believe and trust the Lord. How do we know? It is because "all our righteous acts are like filthy rags" (Isa. 64:6), and the Word declares, "There is no one righteous, not even one" (Rom. 3:10). If you claim that your walk with God is a success, trust me, you have not been walking on your own. Your successful walk in holiness is because God has been carrying you and covering you with His love, grace, and everlasting mercy (see Ps. 118).

"It is of the Lord's mercies that we are not consumed because His compassions fail not. They are new every morning: great is thy faithfulness" (Lam. 3:22-23 KJV), meaning God's faithfulness, not ours. Paul says it is not I but Christ who lives in me. Thus, "The life I now live in the body, I live by faith in the Son of God, who loved me and gave himself for me" (Gal. 2:20). Paul also affirms that he had no righteousness of his own, rather, "that which is through faith in Christ—the righteousness that comes from God on the basis of faith" (Phil. 3:9). But for the grace of God!

After all the years of suffering, the story of Joseph's ascent to the governorship in Egypt is extraordinary. For some, his vindication is sweet. God supernaturally and strategically elevated him to a place commensurate to his character and essential to his divine assignment.

Most of the material researched for this book ends with Joseph in the palace and his family's migration to Egypt, but the story of God's sovereign will does not end there. God is a promise keeper.

The palace and all the activity involving his family in Egypt were the physical or temporal manifestation of Joseph's dreams. However, his dreams had spiritual implications that reached far beyond the palace. They had to do with God's redemptive plan for humanity; thus, they were substantively eternal in nature. Although the full import of his dreams was not imminent, "their historical unfolding spans many generations."[2] The spiritual reality of his dreams continues to this day and has eschatological implications. God is the God of covenant, and He keeps His promises.

In chapter two, I alluded to the fact that Joseph could not die. He could not die because God had a commitment to keep, and God chose Joseph as the vessel to advance or carry forward His promise. Therefore, Joseph had to fulfill every moment of his God-given destiny and purpose on earth. No one could stop God's mission, and no obstacle could prevent this man of God from carrying out God's will.

In her book, *God's Prevailing Truth is Life-Changing*, my dear sister in Christ and powerful woman of God, Reba Manfre teaches that believers should pray daily: "Lord, I thank you that I am on Your timetable, not mine, not the enemy's, and not man's, and not the world's." She continues: "Lord, thank You that I am released into the fulfillment of every second of destiny for which You have put me on this earth."[3]

Joseph was kept and promoted even amid horrible conditions because God had to protect what was in him. The pit was too dark and dingy, Potiphar's house was too messy, and imprisonment for such a violent crime was too final. Consequently, neither the pit, Potiphar's house, nor the prison was a match for God. God kept, preserved, and protected Joseph with surgical precision and laser-like focus. Joseph's final anguish, the prison, is reminiscent of what the enemies of Jesus assumed when He was on the cross. The crowd "stood watching, and the rulers even sneered at Him," and the soldiers "mocked Him" (Lk.23:35-36) as if to say, "it is final, and you are done."

However, God was always at work. We see all the awful things happening to him, but we could not see God's extraordinarily supernatural transformational move within him. We could not see God working out His covenant or performing His promise by preserving Joseph. We saw the human pain but not the Godly prowess. He was destined for the palace from day one. How do we know that? As discussed in chapter nine, we know that because God sent him, absolutely nothing happens outside God's authority. Our sovereign Lord is always in complete control, no matter how grim things appear.

Let me encourage the believer that God knows where you are and what you face. He also knows what He has invested in you: Jesus Christ, "the hope of glory" (Col. 1:27), and He walks and talks with His image-bearers. It is God who keeps your soul (Ps. 25:20), and He has plans for your life that the enemy cannot undermine. "For I know the plans I have for you," declares the Lord, "plans to prosper you and not to harm you, plans to give you hope and a future" (Jer. 29:11). It is God who establishes boundaries and sets parameters, not the enemy, and it is He who orders our every step (Ps.37:23). Remember, God promised.

God never said that this journey would be easy, and no one has claimed that the road of life would not be cumbersome. The vicissitudes of life can become overwhelming, but our Lord does promise to be with us through every mountain and every valley. The promise to the biblical Christian is abundant life, not an easy life (Jn. 10:10). One of my favorite passages is from the Psalms: "I will lift up mine eyes unto the hills, from whence cometh my help. My help cometh from the Lord, which made heaven and earth" (Ps. 121:1-2 KJV).

Wiersbe thoughtfully reminds us, "People with faith are also people with feelings, and feelings must not be discredited or ignored."[4]

Every living and breathing human being experiences a range of emotions from time to time because of feelings of heartache, pain, disappointment, and many others. It is not my desire to minimize or dismiss the most natural of all, which is human emotions. However, my hope and prayer is that we may learn, by God's grace, how to look beyond the pain and problems with an eye of faith toward the promises.

God made a covenant with Joseph's great-grandfather, Abraham, and Joseph's journey, his very life, was inextricably tied to that covenant. Under no circumstance could he have died on his way to the palace. There was no way possible for any of what came upon Joseph to hinder Joseph. In the promises to Abraham, "God has declared an unalterable purpose to accomplish certain ends. There may be delays, postponements, chastisements, and blessings apart from these promises, but the ultimate purpose of God will be fulfilled only by the accomplishment of the promises."[5]

As bleak and dire as things appeared to be, God had a promise to keep, and that promise reached far beyond the palace. Everyone celebrates the happy ending of Joseph in the palace and his rise to the governorship in Egypt. Certainly, his arrival, by the grace of God, is worth celebrating. Still, Joseph's dreams were about the Lord preserving His promise to Abraham throughout eternity. God saved Joseph to save his family, thus, His covenant. Not only could Joseph not die, but his brothers could not die until they, too, fulfilled every moment of their destiny. The dreams within Joseph had to do with God's plan of the redemption of humanity, salvific history, which began with Abraham. Our God keeps His promises.

CHAPTER 11

The Unilateral Covenant with Abraham

Now the Lord had said unto Abram, Get thee out of thy country, and from thy kindred, and from thy father's house, unto a land that I will shew thee: And I will make of thee a great nation, and I will bless thee, and make thy name great; and thou shalt be a blessing: And I will bless them that bless thee, and curse him that curseth thee: and in thee shall all families of the earth be blessed. (Gen. 12:1-3 KJV)

Some writers believe that the Abrahamic covenant is a conditional, thus, bilateral covenant based on Genesis 22. Abraham was willing to offer his son Isaac as a sacrifice. According to the Scripture:

Then God said, "Take your son, your only son, whom you love—Isaac—and go to the region of Moriah. Sacrifice him there as a burnt offering on a mountain I will show you." Early the next morning, Abraham got up and loaded his donkey. He took with him two of his servants and his son Isaac. When he had cut enough wood for the burnt offering, he set out for the place God had told him about. On the third day, Abraham looked up and saw the place in the distance. He said to his servants, "Stay here with the donkey while I and the boy go over there. We will worship, and then we will come back to you." (Gen. 22:2-5)

Abraham obeyed God and was prepared to offer Isaac a sacrifice unto God. However, God intervened:

When they reached the place God had told him about, Abraham built an altar there and arranged the wood on it. He bound his son Isaac and laid him on the altar, on top of the wood. Then he reached out his hand and took the knife to slay his son. But the angel of the Lord called out to him from heaven, "Abraham! Abraham!" "Here I am," he replied. "Do not lay a hand on the boy," he said. "Do not do anything to him. Now I know that you fear God because you have not withheld from me your son, your only son." (Gen. 22:9-12)

The following passage is the passage that raises debate over whether the Abrahamic covenant is unilateral (unconditional) or bilateral (conditional):

The angel of the Lord called to Abraham from heaven a second time and said, "I swear by myself, declares the Lord, that because you have done this and have not withheld your son, your only son, I will surely bless you and make your descendants as numerous as the stars in the sky and as the sand on the seashore. Your descendants will take possession of the cities of their enemies, and through your offspring, all nations on earth will be blessed because you have obeyed me." (Gen. 22:15-18)

Abraham's obedience is extraordinarily praiseworthy. However, those who view the Abrahamic covenant as bilateral or conditional fail to recognize several overarching details.

First, in Genesis 12:1-3, as mentioned above, God was the conversationalist; Abraham did not say a word. Walvoord postulates: "The original promises were given to Abraham without any conditions whatever."[1] Wiersbe agrees that "There were no conditions attached."[2] Over and over, God rehearsed with Abraham what He would do, but Abraham did not verbalize any commitment whatsoever. Never did God condition the seven blessings upon any action of Abraham. So, "the covenant of grace came from the generous heart of God."[3]

Suppose many scholars and theologians are correct that the Abrahamic covenant is based on the condition of Abraham's obedience. In that case, I submit that even his obedience depended upon God's ability to keep him and not Abraham's ability to be obedient. Jesus helps us with this. Jesus proclaims: "I am the vine; you are the branches…apart from me you can do nothing" (Jn.15:5). Jesus said it, and nothing means nothing.

Second, God later repeated the original covenant to Abraham. Again, the promises were unconditional:

> The Lord said to Abram after Lot had parted from him, "Look around from where you are, to the north and south, to the east and west. All the land that you see I will give to you and your offspring forever. I will make your offspring like the dust of the earth so that if anyone could count the dust, then your offspring could be counted. Go, walk through the length and breadth of the land, for I am giving it to you." (Gen. 13:14-17)

Third, well before the Mt. Moriah experience in Genesis 22, again, God formalized or reaffirmed the covenant. Notice, "it was God who made promises to Abraham, not Abraham who made promises to

God."[4] Abraham had questions about how God would pull it off, but he made no promises. According to the Scripture:

> Then the word of the Lord came to him: "This man will not be your heir, but a son who is your own flesh and blood will be your heir." He took him outside and said, "Look up at the sky and count the stars—if indeed you can count them." Then he said to him, "So shall your offspring be." (Gen. 15:4-5)

> But Abram said, "Sovereign Lord, how can I know that I will gain possession of it?" So the Lord said to him, "Bring me a heifer, a goat, and a ram, each three years old, along with a dove and a young pigeon." Abram brought all these to him, cut them in two, and arranged the halves opposite each other; the birds, however, he did not cut in half. Then birds of prey came down on the carcasses, but Abram drove them away. (Gen. 15:8-11)

Fourth, and probably the most salient point, Abraham fell asleep, and God did the work. Hence, "God alone passed between the parts of the sacrifices."[5] In other words, the covenant was "ratified by an oath of God" and God alone.[6] It was solely based on God's faithfulness and not Abraham's obedience or faithfulness to God:

> As the sun was setting, Abram fell into a deep sleep, and a thick and dreadful darkness came over him. Then the Lord said to him, "Know for certain that for four hundred years your descendants will be strangers in a country not their own and that they will be enslaved and mistreated there. But I will punish the nation they serve as slaves, and afterward, they will come out with great possessions. You, however, will go to your ancestors in peace and be buried at a good old age. In the fourth generation, your descendants will come back here, for the sin of the Amorites has not yet reached its full measure." When the sun had set, and darkness had fallen, a smoking firepot with a

blazing torch appeared and passed between the pieces. On that day, the Lord made a covenant with Abram and said, "To your descendants, I give this land, from the Wadi of Egypt to the great river, the Euphrates— the land of the Kenites, Kenizzites, Kadmonites, Hittites, Perizzites, Rephaites, Amorites, Canaanites, Girgashites, and Jebusites." (Gen. 15:12-21)

God initiated the covenant, and God, alone, performed the necessary ceremony required to enact or cut the covenant (see Jer. 34:18-19). There is no question that God intended to uphold both ends. Andrew Murray also gives some insight to those who insist that obedience to God was the condition of the covenant. He correctly notes that God had to train Abraham "to trust Him as the omnipotent One."[7] In other words, whatever obedience Abraham had was by what S. Lewis Johnson calls "the efficacious grace of God."[8] If God were to pull off the provisions of this covenant for generations to come, He certainly had wisdom enough not to depend upon human beings.

Joseph's dreams had implications that reached beyond the palace. They had eternal ramifications. God had promises to keep. He had our redemption in mind from the beginning of time. That God singled out a man who was once "a worshipper of false gods (Joshua 24:2, 3)"[9] called him, and established a covenant which is, as Hester maintains, "the most important religious event since the fall of man," is beyond amazing.[10]

Piper postulates, "...for his own wise purposes, God set his favor on a single man, Abram, and commenced an amazing 2,000-year history that would, in the fullness of time, bring forth Jesus Christ the Redeemer for all the world."[11] Harris posits, "The Bible, from beginning to end, is the development of this grand idea of blessing from God to sinful man through redemption. It lies here in the beginning of the history, in the promise to Abraham, the key to the entire Bible and to all God's action in man's redemption."[12]

Joseph was "the divine means" by which God used to carry out His plans and purposes. God used Joseph to save his family or "to keep the flame alive"[13] and, thus, to bless all the people of the world through Jesus Christ. However, "he is not the son through whom the covenant promise is passed."[14] That call, and covenantal responsibility, God gave to Judah.

Of course, Abraham's physical seed is Isaac,[15] with whom the promise is reaffirmed in Genesis 26. The Word of the Lord says:

> Stay in this land for a while, and I will be with you and will bless you. For to you and your descendants, I will give all these lands and will confirm the oath I swore to your father, Abraham. I will make your descendants as numerous as the stars in the sky and will give them all these lands, and through your offspring, all nations on earth will be blessed. (Gen. 26:3-4)

The blessing is also reaffirmed with Jacob, Isaac's son, in Genesis 28:

> There above it stood the Lord, and he said: "I am the Lord, the God of your father Abraham and the God of Isaac. I will give you and your descendants the land on which you are lying. Your descendants will be like the dust of the earth, and you will spread out to the west and to the east, to the north and to the south. All peoples on earth will be blessed through you and your offspring. (Gen. 28:13-14)

God changed Jacob's name to Israel in Genesis 32. Hence, Jacob, the supplanter, becomes Israel, prince of God[16] or the progenitor of the twelve tribes of Israel:

> Then the man said, "Your name will no longer be Jacob, but Israel because you have struggled with God and with humans and have overcome. (Gen. 32:28)

It is at this point we realize the beginning of a nation as promised in Genesis 12:2: "I will make you into a great nation," and the beginning of God's redemption plan for man in Gen. 12:3: "and in thee shall all families of the earth be blessed" (see also Gen. 22:18).

CHAPTER 12

Beyond the Palace

Although Joseph's story encompasses several themes that give hope to the hopeless and encourage those discouraged, some may underestimate or underappreciate the significance of Joseph's gift and call beyond the palace. Joseph was the precursor or conduit through whom God used to preserve His covenant with Abraham to ensure its enlargement and perpetuation. The Word says:

> Then Jacob left Beersheba, and Israel's sons took their father Jacob and their children and their wives in the carts that Pharaoh had sent to transport him. So Jacob and all his offspring went to Egypt, taking with them their livestock and the possessions they had acquired in Canaan. Jacob brought with him to Egypt his sons and grandsons and his daughters and granddaughters —all his offspring. (Gen. 46:5-7)

If Hester is correct that God's covenantal relationship with Abraham is the most important religious experience since the fall of

Adam and Eve, then as a type of sacrifice, Joseph's role was of utmost significance. Nonetheless, the Abrahamic covenant is essential to understanding the entire history of the Old Testament[1] and God's actions in history.

God used Joseph to save his family from the worldwide famine. However, Joseph could not have known the full import of his divine assignment. Neither could he have known just how comprehensive God's plan was. The Lord was after Joseph. Likewise, the Lord was after his brothers, who would become the twelve tribes of Israel.

Of course, God cares for every living creature in His vast creation. However, as we have witnessed, He was particularly concerned for the survival of Joseph's family,[2] Abraham's descendants. Although God's plan of redemption and reclamation began with Abraham, He always had the world in view. Thus, "He has a plan, a clear purpose for the centuries, and it reaches even to us" to this day.[3]

While the treatment of the Abrahamic covenant will not be exhaustive here, I will attempt to discuss three provisions of the Abrahamic covenant relevant to the purpose of this book.

First, God promised to preserve them a remnant. God used Joseph to further His mission on the earth by preserving them "a remnant on earth" (Gen. 45:7). Little did they know that the very one they wanted to get rid of was the one God would use to save their lives. From the very start, they were his assignment. They were after Joseph, but God was after them. Hence, from the seed of Abraham, a nation (Israel) is born.

Not only did God promise to preserve them a remnant, but second, God promised to make Abraham's name great. The remarkable reality that God chose Abraham and cut covenant with him "to make his posterity God's chosen people, stands there, in its place in the world's history, a revelation of God."[4] He represents "a new creation; a new page of history opens."[5] In fact, the three major monotheistic religions of the world recognize Abraham as the father of faith: Christianity, Judaism, and Islam.[6]

Finally, God promised to bless all families of the earth. Abraham's name is also great because, as Schreiner suggests, in his lineage are "kingly associations."[7] God said to Abraham, "...and kings will come from you" (Gen. 17:6); of Sarah, God said, "...kings of peoples will come from her" (Gen. 17:16). To Jacob, God said, "and kings will be among your descendants" (Gen. 35:11).

Furthermore, Paul says to the church at Galatia, "Now to Abraham and his seed were the promises made," and for clarity, he adds, "He saith not, And to seeds, as of many; but as of one, And to thy seed, which is Christ" (Gal. 3:16 KJV). Thus, the Abrahamic covenant is fulfilled or inaugurated through Jesus Christ: "a righteous Branch" of David, "a king who would reign wisely" (Jer. 23:5), "from the stump of Jesse" (Isa. 11:1). All families of the earth shall be blessed "through the redemption of Jesus Christ,"[8] the seed of Abraham.

Through all his sufferings and trials, God used Joseph to save his family, thereby saving God's plan of redemption, fulfilled in Jesus Christ, making his story one of the most awe-inspiring stories of all times. His work foreshadowed the work of Jesus Christ. As a typology, much like Christ, Joseph was loved by his father, betrayed and rejected by his brothers, falsely accused, and unjustly arrested, but after it all, God raised him to rule over the land, and he could forgive those who wronged him.

When the word seed is used, God refers to a single seed, not seeds, as Paul explains in Galatians 3:16. The promised seed in the lineage of Abraham is Jesus Christ, as recorded in Matthew 1. Hence, Jesus is the seed of Abraham:

> That in blessing I will bless thee, and in multiplying I will multiply thy seed as the stars of the heaven, and as the sand which is upon the sea shore; and thy seed shall possess the gate

of his enemies; And in thy seed shall all the nations of the earth be blessed; because thou hast obeyed my voice. (Gen. 22:17-18 KJV)

Jesus is also the Lion of Judah:

Judah, thou art he whom thy brethren shall praise: thy hand shall be in the neck of thine enemies; thy father's children shall bow down before thee. Judah is a lion's whelp: from the prey, my son, thou art gone up: he stooped down, he couched as a lion, and as an old lion; who shall rouse him up? (Gen. 49:8-9)

Even though God used Joseph to preserve His promise, it was through Judah that "royalty would reside until the Messiah comes."[9] The Word says:

The sceptre shall not depart from Judah, nor a lawgiver from between his feet, until Shiloh come; and unto him shall the gathering of the people be. Binding his foal unto the vine, and his ass's colt unto the choice vine; he washed his garments in wine, and his clothes in the blood of grapes: His eyes shall be red with wine, and his teeth white with milk. (Gen. 49:8-12)

In John's "Revelation of Jesus Christ, which God gave to him" (Rev. 1:1 KJV), the only one found worthy to "open and to read the book" or "look therein" will be Jesus Christ, "the Lion of the Tribe of Judah" (Rev. 5:5 KJV).

Matthew records "The book of the generation of Jesus Christ" and confirms that Jesus is "the son of David, the son of Abraham" (Mt. 1:1 KJV). John not only refers to Christ as the Lion of Judah but also "the Root of David," who "prevailed to open the book and to loose the seven seals thereof" (Rev. 5:5 KJV). Moreover, the prophet Nathan foretells that God would establish His kingdom through King David's physical lineage. Hence, Jesus is the Son of David:

> And as since the time that I commanded judges to be over my people Israel, and have caused thee to rest from all thine enemies. Also, the Lord telleth thee that he will make thee an house. And when thy days be fulfilled, and thou shalt sleep with thy fathers, I will set up thy seed after thee, which shall proceed out of thy bowels, and I will establish his kingdom. He shall build an house for my name, and I will stablish the throne of his kingdom forever. I will be his father, and he shall be my son. If he commit iniquity, I will chasten him with the rod of men, and with the stripes of the children of men: But my mercy shall not depart away from him, as I took it from Saul, whom I put away before thee. And thine house and thy kingdom shall be established forever before thee: thy throne shall be established forever. According to all these words, and according to all this vision, so did Nathan speak unto David. (2 Sam. 7:11-17 KJV)

Paul also affirms that Jesus is the Son (seed) of David:

> Paul, a servant of Jesus Christ, called to be an apostle, separated unto the gospel of God, (Which he had promised afore by his prophets in the holy Scriptures) Concerning his Son Jesus Christ our Lord, which was made of the seed of David according to the flesh; And declared to be the Son of God with power, according to the spirit of holiness, by the resurrection from the dead. (Rom.1:1-3 KJV)

Furthermore, in the isle of Patmos (Rev. 1:9), John saw an opened heaven. Before him stood "a white horse, whose rider is called Faithful and True" (Rev. 19:11). This is who Paul called "the blessed and only Potentate (1 Tim. 6:15 KJV). He will overcome those who "make war with the Lamb" (Rev. 17:14). He saw Jesus, and His name written on "His robe and on His thigh...

King of kings and Lord of Lords" (Rev. 19:16).

This is the immense weight of what Joseph carried, probably unknowingly, from the pit to the palace. It is even more weighty because of its implications beyond the palace in Egypt. Let us not overlook the years of suffering and sacrifice with which he had to contend. God chose and appointed a special people to Himself through whom the entire world would be blessed. His role in preserving his family and, subsequently, the lineage which gave the world God's "only begotten Son that whosoever believeth in him should not perish, but have everlasting life" (Jn. 3:16 KJV) cannot be trivialized.

Although the story of the palace may seem like the climax, it is only the perpetuation of God's ultimate plan and design. What rests beyond Joseph's residence in the palace is the promise God made to his great-grandfather, Abraham. It is the promise of the hope of the reconciliation of a fallen man to a loving and gracious God. Thus, the hope of eternal life through Jesus Christ our Lord.

Everything God did in the life of Joseph and everyone God used in this drama, especially his brothers, was about God's covenantal promise to Abraham, with a particular focus on Jesus Christ, who was the promised seed. It is no small matter; it should inform our faith in God's sometimes invisible yet providential hand. In fact, it means everything to those who believe, receive, and desire eternal life.

Hence, Jesus Christ is the promise; He is God's plan of redemption for humanity and "Mediator of a new covenant" (Heb. 9:15) "established upon better promises" (Heb. 8:6 KJV). It is through Christ that God reconciled the world to Himself (2 Cor. 5:19). Therefore, it was ultimately all about Jesus Christ, our Lord, and our Redeemer who "endured the cross, scorning its shame and sat down at the right hand of the throne of God" (Heb. 12:2).

For "In Him, we have redemption through His blood, the forgiveness of sins, in accordance with the riches of God's grace" (Eph.1:7). "He redeemed us in order that the blessing given to Abraham might come to the Gentiles through Christ Jesus so that by faith we might receive the promise of the Spirit" (Gal. 3:14). Therefore, "If you belong to Christ, then you are Abraham's seed, and heirs according to the promise" (Gal. 3:29). In other words, Christ, the seed of Abraham, died that we might live (2 Cor. 5:15; 1 Thess. 5:10). Now the mystery hidden from all the ages is revealed: "Christ in you, the hope of glory" (Col. 1:27).

That was God's plan from the beginning of time when "He chose us in Him before the foundation of the world" (Eph. 1:4 KJV). The implications of Joseph's dreams reached far beyond the palace. Not only did the preservation of Joseph's family rest in Joseph, but also the progression and propagation of our chosenness.

Joseph's triumphant end should encourage the faithful that God knows exactly what He is doing, why He is doing it, and why He chooses to do it in the manner He does. His unfair treatment at home, unnatural sufferings abroad, the unlikely path to Egypt, and all God accomplished through him reveal to us the invisible hand of God. We may not see Him in the storm, but we know He sees us and is more than able to see us through.

This is God's world, and we are His creation, making Him the universe's owner and sustainer. Therefore, sovereign God has the right to do what pleases Him in the way He chooses. Absolutely nothing happens outside of God's authority, and no matter how things look, sound, or feel, He is in complete control. May we learn to seek His will, trust His plan, and know that He will keep us through life's trials and adversities.

Conclusion

In summary, the life of Joseph was riddled with jealousy, hatred, betrayal, lies, deception, and much more. However, God gave him victory over his enemies in every calamitous situation. God used what they meant for evil to protect Joseph and to promote him to greatness, just as God promised to do in the lives of those who love and trust Him today. Though hurtful, the almost deadly betrayal of his brothers only pushed him into his divine destiny. Potiphar's wife's lies only propelled him to his next level of greatness. Although the butler forgot him for two long years, he remembered Joseph at the perfect time, which speaks to God's divine will and intentionality. On the right day at the right time, Joseph ended up in the presence of the king.

Believers, God can and will use anything He wants to accomplish His plans and purposes. None of the perpetrators could have imagined just how much God would use their evil deeds. He specializes in things that, to human beings, may seem impossible. Whatever the situation, wherever Joseph landed, God allowed him to walk with a special grace that cannot be denied. God gave him a special grace to forget the pain and heartache he had lived through for years. He also gave him a special grace to be fruitful and prosper amid whatever situation or circumstance thrust upon him. Through it all, God graced him to forgive his brothers for their wicked actions against him and his father.

Joseph was broken but not bitter and certainly not destroyed. Their experience in Egypt before Joseph eventually broke his brothers, and God used their brokenness to further His mission. He not only had plans for Joseph; He had plans for his brothers also. Sometimes we cannot discern whom the Lord will use and how He will work out His purposes.

It had to be through divine revelation that Joseph knew it was God from beginning to end. Whatever the enemy meant for evil, Joseph realized that God was using it, and He turned it around in his favor. Thus, it was God all the time; it was all in His plan.

God had a promise to keep. Everything in Joseph's life was connected inexorably to God's promise to his great-grandfather, Abraham. Even though, at times, for Joseph, it looked like impending death or life imprisonment. Nevertheless, God had a covenant to keep that He alone executed between Abraham and Himself. It was a unilateral covenant solely based on God's faithfulness and not Abraham's faithfulness or obedience to God. He did what He always has to do with His created beings; He had to uphold both ends of the relationship. Without Him in our lives, without the gift of His Holy Spirit, we can do absolutely nothing. Even if we manage to do what is honorable or right in His sight, it is only by the enduring grace that God grants us.

While the palace may seem climactic, the implications of Joseph's dreams reach far beyond the Egyptian palace. The story of Joseph rests in the annals of salvific history. God called, used, protected, and promoted Joseph to propagate His mission on earth. That mission was to get Christ on earth so that He may reconcile dying humanity to Himself. God pulled it off.

The eschatological implications of Joseph's dreams are far-reaching, climaxing at the day our Lord shall appear, thus, the final destiny of our souls, our eternal destiny. What does that mean for us today? It means that we, too, are heirs of the Abrahamic covenant. Hence, the implications extend to us today from the preservation and creation of a nation, God's chosen people, to Jesus Christ. And through Jesus Christ, we have the promise of eternal life.

Through life's storms, hurts, and disappointments, God will always work things out in the lives of those who love and serve Him. Nothing happens outside of God's authority, no matter how it feels, looks, or sounds. God is always in complete control over people, situations, and circumstances. His providential hand is at work, and our God is sovereign. May we learn to love and trust Him more and more.

APPENDIX A

THE PROVIDENCE OF GOD

There is the age-old theological question about God's role in human affairs. Bush posits that among many disciplines, science particularly, "nothing is thought of as being outside the natural cause-and-effect system." In other words, "Everything is seen as a part of one vast impersonal system." He further notes a period in which Christianity or orthodoxy gave way to eighteenth and nineteenth-century Deism, which is the theory that although "God had created everything," "He simply left the universe to run by its own natural powers."[1]

Today, the evolution from modernism to postmodernism rules the day. It appears that now, more than ever, people are questioning God's Providence and even challenging God's very existence. This challenge is real, especially as the world wrestles with the COVID-19 pandemic. In the face of this deadly disease, some question how God can, if He exists, merely sit back and allow such evil all over the world.

There are four reasons for treating the subject of providence in this context. First, that people may know Him, the truth of the nature and character of God (Phil 3:10). Second, to defend the faith (1 Pet. 3:15) and to destroy objections raised against the knowledge of God (2 Cor. 10:5). Third, to address the problem of evil in the context of providence. Finally, to provide a clear apologetic framework to edify the body of Christ and to encourage the future study of the Theology of Providence. There is a God who created and sustains His creation by His, sometimes, invisible hand, even in the darkest hour.

THE EXISTENCE OF GOD

The Word of God does not "argue for God's existence. It simply affirms it or, more often, merely assumes it."[2] For the Christian faith, "the basis of authority for knowing reality (God) is the Bible," which is, in essence, "God's written revelation to humanity."[3] God is a self-revealing God, and "the Biblical pronouncement on the existence of God, and all else, is self-attesting or self-authenticating."[4] The Bible was "written by authors divinely inspired and guided by the same self-revealing God. God the Father became incarnate, saving fallen creation, bringing His Kingdom through uniting our humanity to His divine life in the Second Person of the Holy Trinity as the historical man and Son of God Jesus of Nazareth."[5]

In Lewis' view, immanence and transcendence are attributes of God. He asserts that "God is an invisible, personal, and living Spirit, distinguished from all other spirits by several kinds of attributes." He continues, "relationally, God is transcendent in being, immanent universally in providential activity, and immanent with His people in redemptive activity."[6] However, Erickson suggests that "immanence and transcendence should not be regarded as attributes of God." Instead, "transcendence and immanence should be regarded as indications of how God, in all of His attributes, relates to His world."[7]

"God is known only through his initiative in disclosing Himself through revelation."[8] His existence is realized by general[9] and special revelation.[10] However, according to von Wachter, one of the four reasons that Buchheim gives for "doubting the possibility of God's existence" is that "there is no clear concept of God."[11] To the believer, "The most basic conception of God" that biblical Christians "know, is God as Creator." God, not "constrained in his creative act by pre-existent matter," is the "unique source and focus of being." In other words, Creator *ex nihilo*, meaning, "God brought the world into existence out of nothing through the purposeful act of His free will."[12]

"God is the absolute source of everything that is not God (including time and space), and creation is, in itself, nothing."[13] "It is the activity of creation that establishes our deepest and most essential relation to God."[14] Bush asserts, "Human beings are uniquely created in God's image though they are physically a part of nature." Also, "Mankind, in the traditional worldview, is uniquely related to God."[15] Thus, "the doctrine of Providence has generally been treated as a subdivision of the doctrine of creation."[16] It is the Word, through whom all things are made, that lies at the heart of creation as the origin of its existence and order.[17]

THE THEOLOGY OF PROVIDENCE

"The doctrine of Providence has always formed an essential part of the Christian faith."[18] Providence, according to Erickson, is the "continuing action of God by which He preserves in existence the creation He has brought into being and guides it to His intended purpose for it."[19] "The fact that God preserves His creation, guides it into the intelligent and wise consummation of His purposes and governs it as sovereign God, is by its very character essential to true theism."[20]

Although the word Providence does not appear in the Bible, there is the intimation or "reality" of Providence, which does. Thereby, the "reality in the universe" of God's Providence.[21] Fergusson asserts "the Latin word *providebit*," which "appears in Genesis 22:8 where Abraham tells Isaac that God will provide a sacrificial lamb," and "the Greek word *pronoia*," which denotes "divine foresight," is closely linked to notions of provision, rule, guidance, and purpose. However, like Piper, Fergusson agrees that "the term Providence seldom occurs in either the Hebrew Bible or the New Testament."[22] Much like the doctrine of inerrancy, the doctrine of Providence is implicit rather than explicitly taught,[23] notably, general, and specific Providence.

Much discussion has taken place "throughout the history of the church" regarding "general or specific" Providence.[24] According to Ezigbo, "General Providence, also known as general sovereignty, is the view that seeks to preserve God's sovereignty and human (libertarian) freedom." In other words, it is the thought that "God has not ordained or decreed all human actions...human freedom places limitations on God's sovereignty."[25] Or, as Erickson suggests, "God has general goals that He intends and actually attains." Thus, "He permits considerable variance, allowing for human choice,"[26] whereby "placing limitations on God's sovereignty."[27] Erickson suggests that "traditional Arminians," for example, "hold that humans have free will, by which they mean libertarian or non-compatibilist freedom. Meaning free will, and determinism are not compatible. Thus, "God chose to limit Himself."[28]

On the other hand, "Meticulous Providence (also known as specific Providence) is the view that sees God's providential act as involving complete control of human affairs. For this view, God has a purpose for every human action and experience. Nothing happens without God's prior knowledge of it and God's decision to cause it or allow it to happen."[29] Bawulski and Watkins suggest that it is "the idea that God orders all things that come to pass, such that no event occurs without his concurrently bringing it about in conjunction with mundane creaturely causes."[30] Essentially, "God decides even the details of His plan and ensures that they eventuate as He intends."[31]

Ultimately, one must "resist the temptation to think about providence generally and independently of Christ." For "it is in Jesus Christ" that "God has set up the relation-ship between Himself and His creatures."[32] For in Him, all things were created: things in heaven and on earth, visible and invisible, whether thrones, powers, rulers, or authorities; all things have been created through Him and for Him (Col.

1:16 NIV). Ezigbo posits that "we must account for the scriptural teaching on God's sovereignty (God's rule over God's creation) and God's free will—God's ability to create beings with free will and with the capacity to use it." He continues, "we should also account for the Scriptural teaching on God's ability not to allow the actions of God's creatures to thwart God's eschatological purpose,"[33] "promising to carry through His purpose in creation to its triumphal conclusion."[34]

Finally, whether God's Providence is general or specific, hard determinism or soft determinism, biblical theology is clear. Not only is God present and active in human history, but "He is present and active in our lives, prudently preparing for the future."[35]

THE BIBLICAL VIEW

One need only look at the life of such biblical figures as Joseph (Gen. 37-50), King David and King Saul (1 Sam. 16), and the story of Moses and God's chosen people, especially God's role in "the preservation of Israel as a nation,"[36] to discern the hand of God.

While addressing the "men of Athens," the Apostle Paul says, "From one man He made all the nations, that they should inhabit the whole earth; and He marked out their appointed times in history and the boundaries of their lands" (Acts 17:22-26). Proverbs 16:9 declares, "The heart of man plans his way, but the Lord establishes his steps." Tarvard asserts, "The doctrine of divine Providence has held a singular place in Christian doctrine. The Book of Job, and the Book of Jonas, can be read as reflections on the mystery of divine Providence."[37] The omnipresence and omnipotence of God are evidenced "in His control of the course of history."[38]

Erickson posits, "God's faithfulness is demonstrated repeatedly throughout the pages of Scripture." One example is the providential hand of God in the life of Abraham. "His promise to Abraham of a son came when Abraham and Sarah were seventy-five and sixty years of age, respectively." He continues, "the promise was repeated over a twenty-five-year period, but without a sign of the expected heir… Abraham took steps to provide for himself a son. Yet God proved faithful," fulfilling His promise with the birth of Isaac.[39]

The pivotal moment in the life of Abraham is when out of obedience, he offered his promised son Isaac to God as a blood sacrifice. Tarvard suggests that the story is a "paradoxical tale,"[40] and Erickson indicates that a "paradox is a sign of intellectual indigestion."[41] However, it "has become prototypical of God's dealings with His people, on a path that reached its summit in the Crucifixion of Jesus Christ."[42] Nevertheless, the biblical account affirms, and biblical Christians believe, that "God Himself will provide the lamb" (Gen. 22:8) and that, He did. John declares, "Behold the Lamb of God, who takes away the sins of the world" (Jn. 1:9).

HISTORICAL VIEW

S. Lewis Johnson asserts, "History has a beginning in the creation. There is a controlling principle by which history is carried on to its culmination, and that controlling principle is the sovereignty of God in the affairs of men."[43] One school of thought is that "belief in providence pertained to God's promise for the earthly kingdom, but by the end of the patristic period, those hopes had been dashed and replaced with the goal of a Christian empire and the promise of otherworldly life."[44] Hoonhout postulates, "From its beginning, the Christian tradition followed the Biblical example and discussed Providence in terms of God the Creator, and the world as His work and responsibility." He continues, "The early Church fathers held fast to the belief in a provident Creator as they dialectically appropriated and challenged Greek philosophical thought."[45]

For example, Basil of Caesarea saw God not only as a provider but as a protector.[46] Aquinas' thought was that "God's creation of the universe is to be understood as the production of the total existence of being. Since giving being—that is, creating—implies the totality of being, the creature has a relation of total and complete dependence on God." In other words, "God is the primary cause of all things because what God causes is the very existence of all things, without which things would simply not exist."[47]

In Augustine's *De ordine,* he argues that God has not walked away from His creation. In Augustine's words, "that the organic parts of a flea are marvelously fitted and framed, while human life is surrounded and made restless by the inconsistency of countless disorders."[48] Hence, the human problem is not with God's Providence but with fallen man's limited ability to perceive.

The classical or theistic view of Providence, according to Piper, is God's "sovereignty in the service of wise purposes, or providence is wise and purposeful sovereignty."[49] Parker suggests that Providence is "God's gracious outworking of His purpose in Christ, which issues in His dealings with humankind."[50] It is manifested in "distinguishable aspects of His unitary work: preservation and government (authority)."[51]

Appendix B

Postmodernism and the Problem of Evil

Postmodernism

Postmodernists hold that "Nothing is thought of as being outside the natural cause and effect system. Humanity is thought to be simply a product of chance and natural causes."[1] Therefore, as with Deism, man is on his/her own. MacQuarrie postulates that "Postmodernism has been deeply influenced by Nietzsche as well as by Kierkegaard and Buber, but especially, by Nietzsche's proclamation of the death of God. So, most postmodernists agree that there are no absolute foundations or criteria for our beliefs or moral judgments."[2] In other words, "the reality of a transcendent God at best could not be known, and at worst, did not exist at all."[3] Thus, the musings of Kierkegaard, as Garaventa postulates: "The truth (the doctrine) that Christianity announces is, in fact, something paradoxical, if not utterly absurd: God has become a man, the Eternal has become time, the necessary and immutable Being that, as such, cannot come into existence (cannot have a history), came into existence (He has made Himself history)."[4]

Bush avers that to postmodernists, "Humanity's existence is seen strictly as a product of nature's incessant activity, which in earth's fortuitous environment has been characterized by progressive, advancing change and development."[5] He also notes, "Reality, according to Hegel, was, in essence, a synthesis of being and non-being. Thus, reality was dynamically becoming." He concludes, "Nothing is stable."[6]

A further sign of the times is that "many ordinary people in this postmodern era willingly reject what they assume to be Christian beliefs because of their perceived inherent illogicality."[7] This is especially true in terms of the problem of evil.

THE PROBLEM OF EVIL

One of the most significant challenges to the Christian faith, especially the doctrine of Providence, is the problem of evil. "The problem of evil has been one of the greatest objections to theism since theism has been around."[8] The notion is that "if God exists, there should not be evil" in the world "since God would have the power and desire to stop it."[9] "The existence of evil is seen as proof or evidence that there is no all-powerful, all-loving God. If God is all-powerful and all-loving, why does He not eliminate evil?"[10]

However, the problem of evil is not God. "The true problem of evil is the problem of our evil."[11] The Word of the Lord is unambiguous. When God created the heavens and the earth, everything that He created was "very good" (Gen. 1:31). It was "Adam and Eve's disobedience and commission of sin that brought tragic spiritual, physical, and social deprivation to the entire human race."[12] Thus, "God is the source of all that there is," therefore, "Since all that is, comes from God's will as its source, nothing in existence is in itself evil."[13] Ultimately, as Groothuis posits, it is "Man's inhumanity to man"[14] that is the source of evil.

Yet, it remains necessary for theologians to work on answers to the problem of evil. Erickson postulates, "This problem has occupied the attention of some of the greatest minds of the Christian church." Nevertheless, "None of them was able to put the problem to rest finally and completely."[15] However, some scholars and thinkers have attempted to resolve "the problem of evil for a theological system and demonstrate that God is all-powerful, all-loving, and just despite evil's existence." Hence, "a successful theodicy."[16] For example, one theodicy is "openness theology," which "describes a belief in an open, largely undetermined future."[17] The proponents of "openness theology" hold that "we cannot solve the problem of evil without reconsidering the nature of God." According to Groothuis, openness theology "has been advocated in recent years" by such scholars and thinkers as "Gregory Boyd, Clark Pinnock, John Sanders, and others." He continues, "they assert that if God has a strong providential control of history, evil must be attributed to His agency."[18]

Erickson concludes that "a total solution to the problem of evil is beyond human ability." However, he does posit several themes that may help in dealing with the problem of evil. One theme, for example, is "Evil as a necessary accompaniment of the creation of humanity." In other words, "Humans would not be genuinely human without free will. For God to prevent evil, He would have had to make humanity other than it is."[19] Demarest postulates, "To be authentically human, Adam and Eve must have the opportunity to choose between loyalty to God or self."[20] Erickson believes that "Apparently God felt, for reasons that were evident to Him, but that we can only partly understand, that it was better to make human beings than androids."[21]

CONCLUSION

In summary, life's circumstances or adverse situations may cause some to question not only the Providence of God but also challenge His very existence. It may even lend credence to deistic thought. The question of the day, especially now, from all corners of the globe is, where is God? The answer is God is here, and God is there. If fact, God is everywhere. In other words, although God is not trapped in time (transcendent), which He created, He is ever-present (immanent), relating to His creation, His creatures. God discloses Himself by revealing Himself through His living Word. He has revealed Himself through His Son, Jesus Christ. That God created means that He upholds His creation and sustains it by His mighty love and sovereign power.

While the word Providence does not appear in the Bible, as such, the content of God's character and the context of His Word, as seen in God's continual, active guidance, is evidenced in history. Whether revelation or Providence is general or specific, God accomplishes His plans and purposes for His created world. Paul affirms that He created all things for Him and through Him. Thus, no action, be it human evil or spiritual influence, will frustrate or hinder His original purpose for creation. The life of Joseph, King David, and Moses, and especially God's protection and providential hand in the lives of His chosen people, are clear examples of His invisible hand.

Traditional Christian orthodoxy has always viewed Providence from the highest place to begin, creation. Postmodernists have reduced God to the lowest common Creator and now see man as the ultimate reality. More drastic than Deism, postmodernists entertain the thought that perhaps there is no God at all. Human existence is understood as man's intelligence and modern advancement. Nothing in life is inevitable, except that nothing in life is certain. To postmodernists, the Christian faith is illogical and irrational, especially given the existence of unexplained evil in the world.

However, theologians, scholars, and thinkers may find it difficult, and sometimes impossible, to explain the Providence of God in the light of the presence of evil. Still, one's inability to explain it does not negate the reality of God's sovereignty and God's Providential hand. Although God's hand is sometimes invisible, one cannot overlook the fact that the world is not on autopilot. There must be a delicate balance between determinism and Providence; otherwise, one could topple over into error and imbalance. The theology of hard determinism may need adjusting, but one should not discard Providence because of it.

Finally, there is nothing in existence outside of God's sovereign authority. There is a God. He lives, He rules, and He super rules. God has a plan, a plan for the world He created, and ultimately, there is a determined, purpose-driven end. Yes, God, the Creator, sustains the universe, and His providential hand may be seen even through life's ups and downs. To God, be the glory.

NOTES

CHAPTER 1: FROM THE DREAM TO THE PIT

[1] Bezalel Naor, "Joseph and Daniel: Court Jews and Dreamers," *The Jewish Bible Quarterly* 30, no. 1 (2002): 10-16.
[2] Russell Jay Hendel, "Joseph: A Biblical Approach to Dream Interpretation," *The Jewish Bible Quarterly* 39, no. 4 (2011): 231-238.
[3] Ibid.
[4] Ibid.
[5] Kurt Eisen, "Eugene O'Neill's Joseph: A Touch of the Dreamer," *Comparative Drama* 23, no. 4 (1990): 344.

CHAPTER 2: FROM THE PIT TO POTIPHAR'S HOUSE

[1] Charles Haddon Spurgeon, "My Times are in Thy Hand," *The Spurgeon Center*, From the Metropolitan Pulpit (1891) https://www.spurgeon.org/resource-library/sermons/my-times-are-in-thy-hand/#flipbook/.
[2] Focht Caralie, "The Joseph Story: A Trauma-Informed Biblical Hermeneutic for Pastoral Care Providers," *Pastoral Psychology* 69, no. 3 (06, 2020): 209-23, http://ezproxy.liberty.edu/login?qurl=https%3A%2F%2Fwww.proquest.com%2Fscholarly-journals%2Fjoseph-story-trauma-informed-biblical-hermeneutic%2Fdocview%2F2427188157%2Fse-2%3Faccountid%3D12085.

CHAPTER 3: FROM POTIPHAR'S HOUSE TO THE PRISON

[1] Thomas Sowell, "King and the Dream," *Hoover Digest: Research & Opinion on Public Policy*, no. 1 (Winter 2014): 157–59, https://search.ebscohost.com/login.aspx?direct=true&db=asn&AN=94064905&site=ehost-live&scope=site.
[2] Warren W. Wiersbe, *Be Authentic: Exhibiting Real Faith in the Real-World* (Colorado Springs, CO: Victor Books, 1997), 97.
[3] Gary R. Habermas and Michael R. Licona, *The Case for the Resurrection of Jesus* (Grand Rapids, MI: Kregel Publications, 2004), 138.
[4] Millard J. Erickson, *Christian Theology* Third Edition (Grand Rapids, MI: Baker Academic, 2013), 330.
[5] Sandra McCracken, "When God's Hand is Invisible," *Christianity Today* (Washington) 65, no. 3 (2021), 24.

[6] Wiersbe, *Be Authentic*, 97.
[7] Caralie, "The Joseph Story."

CHAPTER 4: FROM THE PRISON TO THE PALACE

[1] Hendel, "Joseph: A Biblical Approach to Dream Interpretation."

CHAPTER 5: THE MIRACLE OF FORGETFULNESS AND FRUITFULNESS

[1] Charles Hadden Spurgeon, "The Peace of God," Metropolitan Tabernacle Pulpit Volume 24, https://www.spurgeon.org/resource-library/sermons/the-peace-of-god/#flipbook/.
[2] John Piper, "My Peace I give You," Sermon preached on June 9, 2012, https://www.desiringgod.org/messages/my-peace-i-give-to-you.
[3] Millard J. Erickson, *Christian Theology*, 362.

CHAPTER 6: AN UNCOMFORTABLE REUNION

[1] Derek Kidner, *Genesis*. Westmont: InterVarsity Press, 2019. ProQuest Ebook Central. Kidner suggests that Jacob's "refusal to part with Benjamin reveals plainly enough what he had come to suspect." Thus, as a father, Jacob could cover their crimes, but "not their character." He knew them, and he knew the rift between them.
[2] Quote by Dr. Martin Luther King, Jr., Xavier University, https://www.xavier.edu/jesuitresource/online-resources/quote-archive1/martin-luther-king-quotes.
[3] Dorothy F. Zeligs, "The Personality of Joseph," *American Imago; a Psychoanalytic Journal for the Arts and Sciences* 12, no. 1 (Spring, 1955): 47, http://ezproxy.liberty.edu/login?qurl=https%3A%2F%2Fwww.proquest.com%2Fscholarly-journals%2Fpersonality-joseph%2Fdocview%2F1289691691%2Fse-2%3Faccountid%3D12085.
[4] Wiersbe, *Be Authentic,* 109.
[5] Matthew Henry, Matthew Henry's Commentary.
[6] Albert Barnes, Barnes' Notes on the Bible.
[7] Wiersbe, *Be Authentic*, 111.
[8] Ibid. 110.
[9] Rob Starner, "Joseph's Suffering: A Model for Christian Life," (June 2015), https://www.sagu.edu/thoughthub/the-paradigmatic-life-of-joseph.

CHAPTER 7: THE ULTIMATE TEST

[1] Written by Ira Stanphill in 1946. https://www.collegeoftheopenbible.com/hymn-history-there-is-room-at-the-cross-for-you.html.

[2] Wiersbe, *Be Authentic*, 113.

[3] Favour C. Uroko and Obiorah M. Jerome, "Tearing of Clothes: A Study of an Ancient Practice in the Old Testament," *Verbum et ecclesia*, 39, no. 1 (2018): 1–8.

[4] Benjamin D. H. Hilbert, "Joseph's Dreams, Part One: From Abimelech to Saul," *Journal for the Study of the Old Testament* 35, no. 3 (2011): 259-283, https://doi.org/10.1177/0309089210386019.

CHAPTER 8: GOD USES BROKENNESS

[1] Gary M. Barker, "Joseph's Loving Forgiveness of His Brothers," *Paso Robles Press*, July 30, 2021, https://pasoroblespress.com/commentary/josephs-loving-forgiveness-of-his-brothers-by-dr-gary-m-barker/.

[2] Charles R. Swindoll, *The Mystery of God's Will: What Does He Want for Me?* (Nashville, TN: W Publishing Group, 1999), 19.

CHAPTER 9: IT WAS GOD ALL THE TIME

[1] Oswald Chambers, *My Utmost for His Highest*, ed. James Reimann (Grand Rapids, MI: Discovery House Publishers, 1992).

[2] Warren W. Wiersbe, *Be Obedient: Learning the Secret of Living by Faith* (Wheaton, IL.: Victor Books, 1991), 23.

[3] Stephen D. Campbell, "The Surety of God's Promises: A Theological Interpretation of Genesis 22," *Biblical Theology Bulletin* 49, no. 3 (2019): 123-131.

[4] Chambers, *My Utmost for His Highest*.

[5] Spurgeon, "My Times are in Thy Hand."

[6] Chambers, *My Utmost for His Highest*.

[7] Erickson, *Christian Theology*, (2013), 217.

[8] G. R. Lewis, "Attributes of God," *Evangelical Dictionary of Theology* Second Edition, ed. Walter A. Elwell (Grand Rapids, MI: Baker Academic, 2001), 499.

[9] Douglas Groothuis, *Christian Apologetics: A Comprehensive Case for Biblical Faith* (Downers Grove, IL: InterVarsity Press, 2011), 79. [10] Ibid., 176.

[11] Royce Gordon Gruenler, "Romans," ed. Walter A. Elwell, *Evangelical Commentary on the Bible* (Grand Rapids MI.: Baker Book House, 1989), 930.

[12] Wiersbe, *Be Obedient: Learning the Secret of Living by Faith*, 23.

[13] Swindoll, *The Mystery of God's Will,* 20-21.
[14] T. C. Ham, "Songs of Brokenness to the Healing God" *Journal of Spiritual Formation and Soul Care.* 9, no. 2 (2016): 233–246.
[15] Swindoll, *The Mystery of God's Will,* 20.
[16] F. H. Klooster, "Sovereignty of God," *Evangelical Dictionary of Theology* Second Edition ed. Walter A. Elwell (Grand Rapids, MI.: Baker Academic, 2001), 1131.

CHAPTER 10: GOD THE PROMISE KEEPER

[1] R. A. Torrey, *The God of the Bible* (New Kensington, PA.: Whitaker House, 1999), 237-238.
[2] Hilbert, "Joseph's Dreams, Part One: From Abimelech to Saul."
[3] Reba Manfre, *God's Prevailing Truth is Life-Changing,* God's Prevailing Truth Ministries, Saginaw, Al 2006), 10-11.
[4] Wiersbe, *Be Obedient,* 44.
[5] John F. Walvoord, "The Fulfillment of the Abrahamic Covenant," *The Bibliotheca Sacra* 102, no. 405 (1945): 27.

CHAPTER 11: THE UNILATERAL COVENANT WITH ABRAHAM

[1] Walvoord, "The Fulfillment of the Abrahamic Covenant," 27.
[2] Wiersbe, *Be Obedient,* 50.
[3] Ibid.
[4] Ibid.
[5] Ibid.
[6] Walvoord, "The Fulfillment of the Abrahamic Covenant."
[7] Andrew Murray, Absolute Surrender: How to Walk in Perfect Peace, (New Kensington, PA.: Whitaker House, 1982), 71.
[8] S. Lewis Johnson, "The Doctrine of Efficacious and Irresistible Grace," *SLJ Institute,* https://sljinstitute.net/systematic-theology/soteriology/the-doctrine-of-efficacious-and-irresistible-grace/. Dr. S. Lewis was a conservative evangelical pastor and theologian and was for many years a professor at Dallas Theological Seminary.
[9] John Piper, "The Covenant of Abraham," *Desiring God,* https://www.desiringgod.org/messages/the-covenant-of-abraham.
[10] H. I. Hester, *The Heart of Hebrew History: A Study of the Old Testament* (Nashville, TN.: Broadman Press, 1962), 87.
[11] Piper, "The Covenant of Abraham."
[12] Samuel Harris, "Marks of the Supernatural in God's Promise to Abraham," *The Bibliotheca Sacra* 22, no. 85 (1865): 79.
[13] Victor P. Hamilton, "Genesis," ed. Walter A. Elwell, *Evangelical Commentary on the Bible* (Grand Rapids, MI.: Baker Book House Company, 1989), 34.

[14] Ibid.

[15] Walvoord, "The Fulfillment of the Abrahamic Covenant." Walvoord notes that "It was given a visible symbol in the rite of circumcision (Gen. 17:9-14). It was confirmed by the birth of Isaac, by the reiterated promises given to Isaac (Gen. 17:19)."

[16] Hester, *The Heart of Hebrew History*.

CHAPTER 12: BEYOND THE PALACE

[1] Harris, "Marks of the Supernatural in God's Promise to Abraham," 79.

[2] Bruce C. Birch, Walter Brueggemann, Terence E. Fretheim, & David L. Petersen, *A Theological Introduction to the Old Testament* Second Edition (Nashville, TN.: Abingdon Press, 2005), 90.

[3] Piper, "The Covenant of Abraham."

[4] Harris, "Marks of the Supernatural in God's Promise to Abraham," 79.

[5] Iulian Faraoanu, "Abraham's Faith in and Obedience to God," *Romanian Journal of Artistic Creativity* 6, no. 1 (Spring, 2018): 49-58, http://ezproxy.liberty.edu/login?qurl=https%3A%2F%2Fwww.proquest.co m%2Fscholarly-journals%2Fabrahams-faith-obedience-god%2Fdocview%2F2123019992%2Fse-2%3Faccountid%3D12085.

[6] Winfried Corduan, *Neighboring Faiths: A Christian Introduction to World Religions* Second Edition (Downers Grove, IL.: InterVarsity Press, 2012).

[7] Thomas R. Schreiner, *The King in His Beauty: A Biblical Theology of the Old and New Testament* (Grand Rapids, MI.: Baker Academics, 2013), 17.

[8] Walvoord, "The Fulfillment of the Abrahamic Covenant," 27.

[9] Howard F. Vos, *Genesis*, (Chicago, IL: Moody Press, 1982), 166.

APPENDIX A: THE PROVIDENCE OF GOD

[1] L. Russ Bush, *The Advancement: Keeping the Faith in an Evolutionary Age* (Nashville, TN: B&H Publishing Group, 2003), 43-44.

[2] Erickson, *Christian Theology* 1983, 271.

[3] Groothuis, *Christian Apologetics*, 79.

[4] Ibid., 176.

[5] Steve Blakemore, "The Self-Revealing God," *Wesley Biblical Seminary*, (June 21, 2017), accessed August 13, 2020, https://wbs.edu/self-revealing-god/.

[6] G. R. Lewis, "Attributes of God," in *Evangelical Dictionary of Theology Second Edition*, ed. Walter A. Elwell (Grand Rapids: Baker Academic, 2001), 492.

[7] Erickson, *Christian Theology* 2013, 274.

[8] R. L. Saucy, "Doctrine of God," in *Evangelical Dictionary of Theology Second Edition*, ed. Walter A. Elwell (Grand Rapids: Baker Academic, 2001), 500-504.

[9] B. Demarest, General Revelation, "General Revelation," in *Evangelical Dictionary of Theology Second Edition*, ed. Walter A. Elwell (Grand Rapids: Baker Academic, 2001), 1019-1021.

[10] C. F. H. Henry, "Special Revelation," in *Evangelical Dictionary of Theology Second Edition*, ed. Walter A. Elwell (Grand Rapids: Baker Academic, 2001), 1021-1023.

[11] Daniel von Wachter, "Has Modernity Shown All Arguments for the Existence of God to be Wrong?" *Journal of Reformed Theology* 10: 3 (2016), accessed August 13, 2020, doi:10.1163/15697312-01003002.

[12] D. K. McKim, "Doctrine of Creation," in *Evangelical Dictionary of Theology Second Edition*, ed. Walter A. Elwell (Grand Rapids: Baker Academic, 2001), 304.

[13] Simon Oliver, "Augustine on Creation, Providence, and Motion," *International Journal of Systematic Theology* 18: 4 (2016), accessed August 13, 2020, doi:10.1111/ijst.12171.

[14] McKim, "Doctrine of God," 304.

[15] Bush, *The Advancement*, 43-44.

[16] David Fergusson, "The Theology of Providence," *Theology Today* 67: 3 (2010), accessed July 24, 2020, doi:10.1177/004057361006700302.

[17] Ignacio Silva, "Revisiting Aquinas on Providence and Rising to the Challenge of Divine Action in Nature," *The Journal of Religion*, 94: 3 (2014), accessed August 17, 2020, doi:10.1086/676024.

[18] John F Walvoord, *Jesus Christ Our Lord* (Chicago: Moody Publishers 1969), 48.

[19] Erickson, *Christian Theology*, 2013, 359.

[20] Walvoord, *Jesus Christ Our Lord*, 48.

[21] John Piper, "Are God's Providence and God's Sovereignty the Same?" Desiring God, October 18, 2019, accessed August 14, 2020, https://www.desiringgod.org/interviews/are-gods-providence-and-gods-sovereignty-the-same.

[22] Fergusson, "The Theology of Providence."

[23] P. D. Feinberg, "Inerrancy and Infallibility of the Bible," in *Evangelical Dictionary of Theology Second Edition*, ed. Walter A. Elwell (Grand Rapids: Baker Academic, 2001), 159.

[24] Erickson, *Christian Theology*, 2013, 369.

[25] Victor I. Ezigbo, "Divine Providence," in *Introducing Christian Theologies Volume 1: Voices from Global Christian Communities,* (Cambridge: Lutterworth Press, 2013), 222.

[26] Erickson, *Christian Theology*, 2013, 369.

[27] Ezigbo, "Divine Providence," 222.

[28] Erickson, *Christian Theology*, 2013, 369.

[29] Ezigbo, "Divine Providence," 219.

[30] S. Bawulski and James Watkins, "Possible Worlds and God's Creative Process: How a Classical Doctrine of Divine Creation Can Understand Divine Creativity," *Scottish Journal of Theology* 65: 2 (2012), accessed August 18, 2020, http://ezproxy.liberty.edu/login?qurl=https%3A%2F%2Fsearch.proquest.com%2Fdocview%2F963352692%3Faccountid%3D12085.

[31] Erickson, *Christian Theology*, 2013, 369.

[32] T. H. L. Parker, "Providence of God," in *Evangelical Dictionary of Theology* Second Edition, ed. Walter A. Elwell (Grand Rapids: Baker Academic, 2001), 965.

[33] Ezigbo, "Divine Providence," 225.

[34] Parker, "Providence of God," 965.

[35] Erickson, *Christian Theology*, 2013, 359.

[36] Ibid., 360.

[37] George H. Tarvard, "The Mystery of Divine Providence," *Theological Studies* 64: 4 (2003), accessed July 29, 2020, http://ezproxy.liberty.edu/login?qurl=https%3A%2F%2Fsearch.proquest.com%2Fdocview%2F212685453%3Faccountid%3D12085.

[38] Erickson, *Christian Theology*, 2013, 247.

[39] Ibid., 262.

[40] Tarvard, "The Mystery of Divine Providence."

[41] Erickson, *Christian Theology*, 2013, 129.1

[42] Tarvard, "The Mystery of Divine Providence."

[43] S. Lewis Johnson, "Divine Providence, or Is History out of Control?" SLJ Institute (2007), accessed August 19, 2020, https://sljinstitute.net/.

[44] Michael T. Dempsey, "The Politics of Providence in the Early Church: Toward a Contemporary Interpretation," *academia.edu* (2016), accessed August 16, 2020, https://www.academia.edu/.

[45] Michael A. Hoonhout, "Grounding Providence in the Theology of the Creator: The Exemplarity of Thomas Aquinas," *The Heythrop Journal* 43.1 (2002), accessed August 16, 2020, https://doi-org.ezproxy.liberty.edu/10.1111/1468-2265.00179.

[46] Tarvard, "The Mystery of Divine Providence."

[47] Silva, "Revisiting Aquinas On Providence."

[48] Saint Augustine, *The Happy Life; Answer to Skeptics; Divine Providence and the Problem of Evil; Soliloquies*, (Baltimore: Catholic University of America Press, 2008), 240.

[49] Piper, "Are God's Providence and God's Sovereignty the Same?"

[50] Parker, "Providence of God," 965.

[51] Erickson, *Christian Theology*, 2013, 360-365.

APPENDIX B: POSTMODERNISM AND THE PROBLEM OF EVIL

[1] Bush, *The Advancement*, 21.

[2] J. MacQuarrie, "Postmodernism in Philosophy for Religion and Theology," *International Journal for Philosophy of Religion* 50: 1/3 (2001), accessed August 14, 2020, https://doi-org.ezproxy.liberty.edu/10.1023/A:1012050017002.

[3] S. N. Gundry, "Death of god Theology," in *Evangelical Dictionary of Theology* Second Edition, ed. Walter A. Elwell (Grand Rapids: Baker Academic, 2001), 326-327.

[4] Garaventa, Roberto, "Kierkegaard and Christianity: The Difficulty of Communication," *Rivista Di Filosofia Neo-Scolastica* 105: 3/4 (2013), accessed August 17, 2020, http://www.jstor.org/stable/43064091.

[5] Bush, *The Advancement*, 48.

[6] Ibid., 50.

[7] Paul Cudby, "Openness Theology: A New Evangelical Approach to the Epicurean Paradox," *Modern Believing* 46: 2 (2005), accessed August 18, 2020, doi:10.3828/MB.46.2.13.

[8] Gregory E. Ganssle, "The Problem of Evil," *Graduate Resources Web site.* (February 2, 1998), accessed August 14, 2020, https://gradresources.org/579-2/.

[9] Groothuis, *Christian Apologetics*, 615.

[10] Ganssle, "The Problem of Evil."

[11] William Lane Craig, *"Reasonable Faith"*. n.d., accessed August 14, 2020, https://www.reasonablefaith.org/writings/popular-writings/existence-nature-of-god/the-problem-of-evil/.

[12] B. Demarest, "Fall of the Human Race," in *Evangelical Dictionary of Theology Second Edition*, ed. Walter A. Elwell (Grand Rapids: Baker Academic, 2001), 434.

[13] McKim, "Doctrine of Creation."

[14] Groothuis, *Christian Apologetics*, 615.

[15] Erickson, *Christian Theology*, 2013, 386.

[16] J. S. Feinberg, "Theodicy," in *Evangelical Dictionary of Theology Second Edition*, ed. Walter A. Elwell (Grand Rapids: Baker Academic, 2001), 1184-1187.

[17] Cudby, "Openness Theology."

[18] Groothuis, *Christian Apologetics*, 57-58.

[19] Erickson, *Christian Theology*, 2013, 394-365.

[20] Demarest, "Fall of the Human Race," 435.

[21] Erickson, *Christian Theology*, 2013, 395.

BIBLIOGRAPHY

Augustine. 2008. *The Happy Life: Answers to Skeptics; Divine Providence and The Problem of Evil; Soliloquies*. Baltimore: Catholic University of America Press.

Baker, Gary M. 2021. "Joseph's Loving Forgiveness of His Brothers." *Paso Robles Press*.

Bawulski, Shawn, and James Watkins. 2012. "Possible Worlds and God's Creative Process: How a Classical Doctrine of Divine Creation Can Understand Divine Creativity." *Scottish Journal of Theology* 174-191. Accessed August 18, 2020. http://ezproxy.liberty.edu/login?qurl=https%3A%2F%2Fsearch.proquest.com%2Fdocview%2F963352692%3Faccountid%3D12085.

Blackmore, Steve. 2017. "The Self-Revealing God." *Wesley Biblical Seminary*. June 21. Accessed August 13, 2020. https://wbs.edu/self-revealing-god/.

Bruce, Burch c., Walter Brueggemann, Terence E. Fretheim, and David L. Petersen. 2005. *A Theological Introduction to the Old Testament Second Edition*. Nashville: Abingdon Press.

Bush, L. Russ. 2003. *The Advancement: Keeping the Faith in an Evolutionary Age*. Nashville: B&H Publishing Group.

Campbell, Stephen D. 2019. "The Surety of God's Promises: A Theological Interpretation of Genesis 22." *Biblical Theology Bulletin* 49 (3): 123-131.

Caralie, Focht. 2020. "The Joseph Story: A Trauma-Informed Biblical Hermeneutic for Pastoral Care Providers." *Pastoral Psychology* 69 (3): 209-23.

Chambers, Oswald. 1992. *My Utmost for His Highest*. Edited by James Reimann. Grand Rapids: Discovery House Publishers.

Corduan, Winfried. 2012. *Neighboring Faiths: A Christian Introduction to World Religions Second Edition*. Downers Grove: InterVarsity Press.

Craig, William Lane. n.d. "About Us: Reasonable Faith." *Reasonable Faith*. Accessed August 14, 2020. doi:https://www.reasonablefaith.org/writings/popular-writings/existence-nature-of-god/the-problem-of-evil/.

Cudby, Paul. 2005. "Openness Theology: A New Evangelical Approach to the Epicurean Paradox." *Modern Believing* 46 (2): 13-21. Accessed August 18, 2020. doi:10.3828/MB.46.2.13.

Demarest, B. 2001. "Fall of the Human Race." In *Evangelical Dictionary of Theology Second Edition*, by Walter A. Elwell, 434-436. Grand Rapids: Baker Academic.

Demarest, B. 2001. "General Revelation." In *Evangelical Dictionary of Theology Second Edition*, by Walter A. Elwell, 1019-1021. Grand Rapids: Baker Academic.

Dempsey, Michael T. 2016. "The Politics of Providence in the Early Church: Toward a Contemporary Interpretation." *Academia.edu*. Accessed August 17, 2020. https://www.academia.edu/.

Eisen, Kurt. 1990. "Eugene O'Neill's Joseph: A Touch of the Dreamer." *Comparative Drama* 23 (4): 344.

Erickson, Millard J. 1983. *Christian Theology*. Grand Rapids: Baker Academic.

—. 2013. *Christian Theology* Third Edition. Grand Rapids: Baker Academic.

Ezigbo, Victor I. 2013. "Divine Providence." In *Introducing Christian Theologies, Volume 1: Voices from Global Christian Communities*, 218-267. Lutterworth Press. Accessed August 18, 2020.

Faraoanu, Iulian. 2018. "Abraham's Faith in and Obedience to God." *Romanian Journal of Artistic Creativity* 6 (1): 49-58.

Feinberg, J. S. 2001. "Theodicy." In *Evangelical Dictionary of Theology Second Edition*, by Walter A. Elwell, 1184-1187. Grand Rapids: Baker Academic.

Feinberg, P. D. 2001. "Inerrancy and Infallibility of the Bible." In *Evangelical Dictionary of Theology Second Edition*, by Walter A. Elwell, 156-159. Grand Rapids: Baker Academic.

Fergusson, David. 2010. "The Theology of Providence." *Theology Today* 67 (3): 261-278. Accessed July 24, 2020. doi:10.1177/004057361006700302.

Ganssle, Gregory E. 1998. "The Problem of Evil." *Graduate Resources*. February 2. Accessed August 14, 2020. https://gradresources.org/579-2/.

Garaventa, Roberto. 2013. "Kierkegaard and Christianity: The Difficulty of Communication." *Rivista Di Filosofia Neo-Scolastica* 491-503. Accessed August 17, 2020. http://www.jstor.org/stable/43064091.

Gruenler, Royce Gordon. 1989. "Romans." In *Evangelical Commentary on the Bible*, by Walter A. Elwell, 930. Grand Rapids: Baker Book House.

Groothuis, Douglas. 2011. *Christian Apologetics: A Comprehensive Case for Biblical Faith.* Downers Grove: InterVarsity Press.

Gundry, S. N. 2001. "Death of God Theology." In *Evangelical Dictionary of Theology Second Edition*, by Walter A. Elwell, 326-327. Grand Rapids: Baker Academics.

Habermas, Gary R., and Michael R. Licona. 2004. *The Case for the Resurrection of Jesus.* Grand Rapids: Kregel Publications.

Ham, T. C. 2016. "Songs of Brokenness to the Healing God." *Journal of Spiritual Formation and Soul Care* 9 (2): 233-246.

Hamilton, Victor P. 1989. "Genesis." In *Evangelical Commentary on the Bible*, by Walter A. Elwell, 34. Grand Rapids: Baker Book House Company.

Harris, Samuel. 1865. "Marks of the Supernatural in God's Promise to Abraham." *The Bibliotheca Sacra* 22 (85): 79.

Hendel, Russell Jay. 2011. "Joseph: A Biblical Approach to Dream Interpretation." *The Jewish Bible Quarterly* 39 (4): 231-238.

Henry, C. F. H. 2001. "Special Revelation." In *Evangelical Dictionary of Theology Second Edition*, by Walter A. Elwell, 10211023. Grand Rapids: Baker Academic.

Hester, H. L. 1949. *The Heart of Hebrew History: A Study of the Old Testament.* Nashville: Broadman Press.

Hilbert, Benjamin D. H. 2011. "Joseph's Dreams, Part One: From Abimelech to Saul." *Journal for the Study of the Old Testament* 35 (3): 259-283.

Hoonhout, Michael A. 2002. "Grounding Providence in the Theology of the Creator: The Exemplarity of Thomas Aquinas." *The Heythrop Journal* 43 (1): 1-19. Accessed August 16, 2020. https://doi-org.ezproxy.liberty.edu/10.1111/1468-2265.00179.

Johnson, S. Lewis. 2007. *Divine Providence, or Is History Out of Control?* Dallas. Accessed August 19, 2020. https://sljinstitute.net/.

Johnson, S. Lewis. n.d. "The Doctrine of Efficacious and Irresistible Grace." *SLJ Institute.*

Kidner, Derek. 2019. *Genesis.* Westmont: ProQuest Ebook Central.

Klooster, F. H. 2001. "Sovereignty of God." In *Evangelical Dictionary of Theology Second Edition*, by Walter A. Elwell, 1131-1132. Grand Rapids: Baker Academic.

Lewis, G. R. 2001. "Attributes of God." In *Evangelical Dictionary of Theology Second Edition*, by Walter A. Elwell, 492-499. Grand Rapids: Baker Academic.

Macquarrie, J. 2001. "Postmodernism in Philosophy for Religion and Theology." *International Journal for Philosophy of Religion* 50 (1/3): 9-28. Accessed August 14, 2020. https://doi-org.ezproxy.liberty.edu/10.1023/A:1012050017002.

Manfre, Reba. 2006. *God's Prevailing Truth is Life-Changing.* Saginaw: God's Prevailing Truth Ministries.

McCracken, Sandra. 2021. "When God's Hand is Invisible." *Christianity Today* 65 (3): 24.

McKim, D. K. 2001. "Doctrine of Creation." In *Evangelical Dictionary of Theology Second Edition*, by Walter A. Elwell, 304-306. Grand Rapids: Baker Academic.

Murray, Andrew. 1982. *Absolute Surrender: How to Walk in Perfect Peace.* New Kensington: Whitaker House.

Naor, Bezalel. 2002. "Joseph and Daniel: Court Jews and Dreamers." *The Jewish Bible Quarterly* 30 (1): 10-16.

Oliver, Simon. 2016. "Augustine on Creation, Providence, and Motion." *International Journal of Systematic Theology* 18 (4): 379-398. Accessed August 13, 2020. doi:10.1111/ijst.12171.

Parker, T. H. L. 2001. "Providence of God." In *Evangelical Dictionary of Theology Second Edition*, by Walter A. Elwell, 964-965. Grand Rapids: Baker Academic.

Piper, John. 2019. "Are God's Providence and God's Sovereignty the Same?" *Desiring God.* October 18. Accessed August 14, 2020. https://www.desiringgod.org/interviews/are-gods-providence-and-gods-sovereignty-the-same.

Piper, John. 2012. "My Peace I Give You." *Desiring God.*

Piper, John. n.d. "The Covenant of Abraham." *Desiring God.* https://www.desiringgod.org/messages/the-covenant-of-abraham.

Saucy, R. L. 2001. "Doctrine of God." In *Evangelical Dictionary of Theology Second Edition*, by Walter A. Elwell, 500-504. Grand Rapids: Baker Academic.

Schreiner, Thomas R. 2013. *The King in His Beauty: A Biblical Theology of the Old and New Testaments.* Grand Rapids: Baker Academic.

Silva, Ignacio. 1014. "Revisiting Aquinas On Providence and Rising to the Challenge of Divine Action in Nature." *The Journal of Religion* 94 (3): 277-291. Accessed August 17, 2020. doi:doi:10.1086/676024.

Sowell, Thomas. 2014. "King and the Dream." *Hoover Digest: Research & Opinion on Public Policy* (1): 157-59.

Spurgeon, Charles Hadden. 1878. "The Peace of God." *Metropolitan Tabernacle Pulpit* 24.

Spurgeon, Charles Haddon. 1891. *About Us: The Spurgeon Center.*

Starner, Rob. 2015. "Joseph's Suffering: A Model for Christian Life." *Thought Hub.* Southwestern Assemblies of God University.

Swindol, Charles R. 1999. *The Mystery of God's Will: What Does He Want for Me?* Nashville: E-Publishing Group.

Tarvard, George H. 2003. "The Mystery of Divine Providence." *Theological Studies* 64 (4): 707-718. Accessed July 29, 2020. http://ezproxy.liberty.edu/login?qurl=https%3A%2F%2Fsearch.proquest.com%2Fdocview%2F212685453%3Faccountid%3D12085.

The Center for Mission and Identity at Xavier University. n.d. *Jesuit Resource.*

Torrey, R. A. 1999. *The God of the Bible.* New Kensington: Whitaker House.

Uroko, Favour C, and Obiorah M Jerome. 2018. "Tearing of Clothes: A Study of an Ancient Practice in the Old Testament." *Verbum et ecclesia* 39 (1): 1-8.

von Wachter, Daniel. 2016. "Has Modernity Shown All Arguments for the Existence of God to be Wrong?" *Journal of Reformed Theology* 10 (3): 257-61. Accessed August 13, 2020. doi:10.1163/15697312-01003002.

Vos, Howard F. 1982. *Genesis.* Chicago: Moody Press.

Walvoord, John F. 1969. *Jesus Christ Our Lord.* Chicago: Moody Publishers.

Walvoord, John F. 1945. "The Fulfillment of the Abrahamic Covenant." *The Bibliotheca Sacra* 102 (405): 27.

Wiersbe, Warren. 1997. *Be Authentic: Exhibiting Real Faith in the Real-World.* Colorado Springs: Victor Books.

Wiersbe, Warren W. 1991. *Be Obedient: Learning the Secret of Living by Faith.* Wheaton: Victor Books.

Zeligs, Dorothy. 1955. "The Personality of Joseph." *American Imago; A Psychoanalytic Journal for the Arts and Sciences* 12 (1).

ABOUT THE AUTHOR

Clayton D. Smith is the proud founding pastor of Bread of Life Church (Birmingham, Alabama/Albany, Georgia). He has been in Christian ministry for over 40 years serving as a minister of music, administrator, pastor, ministry consultant, and overseer for several churches and ministries. He is the chairman of the Bread of Life Mission Board and serves as CEO of St. Peter's High School, Gardnersville-Monrovia, Liberia, Africa. Brother Smith is an Interdisciplinary Studies Graduate with High Distinction from Liberty University, Lynchburg, Virginia. He is married to Chrystal Smith and has five children.

CPSIA information can be obtained
at www.ICGtesting.com
Printed in the USA
BVHW051220040523
663580BV00017B/828